Three Days of Rain
The American Plan
The Author's Voice
Hurrah at Last

RICHARD GREENBERG

Three Days of Rain
The American Plan
The Author's Voice
Hurrah at Last

Grove Press
New York

Published simultaneously in Canada
Printed in the United States of America

Library of Congress Cataloging-in-Publication Data
Greenberg, Richard, 1958–
Three days of rain and other plays / Richard Greenberg.
    p.   cm.
Contents: Three days of rain—The American plan—The author's
voice—Hurrah at last.
ISBN 0-8021-3636-2
    I. Title
PS3557.R3789T48   1999
812'.54—dc21   99-33515
                              CIP

Grove Press
841 Broadway
New York, NY 10003

03 04 05 06 07 10 9 8 7 6 5 4 3

"Three Days of Rain"

was originally produced in New York City by The Manhattan Theatre Club on October 21, 1997

Commissioned and first produced by South Coast Repertory

"The American Plan"

was originally produced at The Manhattan Theatre Club on January 23, 1990

"The Author's Voice"

was originally presented as part of Marathon '87 at the Ensemble Studio Theater in New York City on May 13, 1987

"Hurrah at Last"

was originally produced in New York City by the Round-about Theater Company on June 3, 1999. Commissioned and first produced by South Coast Repertory.

Contents

Three Days of Rain

For Peter Hedges

Three Days of Rain was commissioned and originally produced by South Coast Repertory and was produced by Manhattan Theatre Club (Lynne Meadow, Artistic Director; Barry Grove, Executive Director) in New York City, on October, 1997. It was directed by Evan Yionoulis; the set design was by Chris Barreca; the costume design was by Candice Cain; the lighting design was by Donald Holder; the sound design was by Red Ramona; the original music was by Mike Yionoulis; the special effects were by Gregory Meeh; and the production stage manager was Roy Harris. The cast was as follows:

Walker/Ned John Slattery
Nan/Lina Patricia Clarkson
Pip/Theo Bradley Whitford
Note: Lina rhymes with Carolina

Setting

Act One

An unoccupied loft space in downtown Manhattan. 1995.

Act Two

The same space, only tenanted and happier. 1960.

Act One

1995

Setting: a somewhat dilapidated, spartanly furnished apartment located on a winding street in downtown Manhattan. Also a portion of that street.

Middle of the night.

Lights are dim.

A low hum of traffic. Walker is lying on the bed, eyes closed, listening. A car alarm sounds, abruptly shuts off. Walker opens his eyes.

Walker Meanwhile, back in the city. . . . Two nights of insomnia. In this room, in the dark . . . listening . . . soaking up the Stravinsky of it. . . . No end to the sounds in a city. . . . Something happens somewhere, makes a noise, the noise travels, charts the distance: The Story of a Moment.

God, I need to sleep! (*He lets out a breath, takes in the room.*)

Yes. All right. Begin. (*Lights fill in. Walker addresses us.*)

My name is Walker Janeway. I'm the son of Edmund Janeway, whose slightly premature death caused such a stir last year, I'm told.

As you're probably aware, my father, along with that tribe of acolytes who continue to people the firm of Wexler Janeway, designed all—yes, *all*—of the most famous buildings of the last thirty years. You've seen their pictures, you may have even visited a few. That Shi`ite Mosque in Idaho. The new library in Bruges. The crafts museum in Austin, that hospice I forget where, and a vertical mall in Rhode Island that in square footage actually exceeds the *state* of Rhode Island.

Years and years and years ago, with his late partner, Theodore Wexler, my father also designed three or four buildings that truly *are* distinguished, chief among them: Janeway House.

I know you know that one.

Everyone's seen that one picture, *LIFE Magazine,* April of '63, I think, where it looks lunar, I mean, like something carved from the moon, mirage-y—you remember that photo? It's beautiful, isn't it? It won some kind of non-Pulitzer Prize that year. People have sometimes declined my invitation to see the real place for fear of ruining the experience of the photograph.

Well. The real place, as it happens, is a private home out in the desirable part of Long Island. My grandparents commissioned it of my father, using all the money they had in the world, because, I guess, they loved him so much. Apparently, there was something there for a parent to love. Hard to imagine how they could tell, though, since he seldom actually spoke. Maybe he was lovable in a Chaplinesque way. Whatever, their faith paid off. The house is now deemed, by those who matter, to be one of the great private residences of the last half-century.

It's empty now.

My sister and I will inherit it today.

We'll be the only family present. Unless you count our friend, Pip, who is my late father's late partner's torpid son.

My mother would be with us, too, of course, but she's, um, like, well, she's sort of like Zelda Fitzgerald's less stable sister, so she can't be there. She's elsewhere, she's . . .

So, then, this is the story as I know it so far:

My father was more-or-less silent; my mother was more-or-less mad. They married because by 1960 they had reached a certain age and they were the last ones left in the room.

And then they had my sister who is somehow *entirely* sane.

And then they had me.

And my father became spectacularly successful, and his partner died shockingly young, and my mother grew increasingly mad, and my sister and I were there so we had to grow up.

   And today we receive our legacy. (*Lights. Nan just arriving.*) You're here!

Nan Yes—

Walker How are you? You look great.

Nan Thank you.

Walker What a relief.

Nan (*Taking the place in.*) Is this where you're *living*?

Walker I had this image of—I was so afraid you were going to look like one of those women, you know, with a wedge cut who are forever eating oriental chicken salads in mall restaurants and going to musicals, but you *don't*, thank God!

Nan You were supposed to meet me.

Walker I—what?

Nan You said you'd—the *plan* was you'd meet me at the airport—

Walker Did we say that?—

Nan I took a cab, finally, when I realized waiting was a lost cause—

Walker I'm—what an idiot!

Nan Yes.

Walker I'm sorry.

Nan Well. You look thin.

Walker Oh, no—

Nan Ectomorph—*plas*mic, almost—are you eating?

Walker Oh God, I'm a *maw*, carbo-loading like a long-distance—well, actually, no, not in the last three days, *two* days—I tried to get a hamburger before but it didn't work out.

Nan I don't know what that means.

Walker I went into this restaurant, sat myself down, and asked for a bacon-cheeseburger, please—I was just so exactly like people, you would have—but then, the waiter? He said: "Thank you. And if you need anything, my name is Craig." So I said: "And if I *don't* need anything, what will your name be?" And he gave me this . . . really annihilating—I had to leave. *I thought I'd said it to myself!* I think maybe I'm not a people person anymore. I've missed you so much.

Nan Aren't we running late?

Walker Not at all—

Nan Will Pip be meeting us here or at—

Walker He's meeting us at Lawyer Fisher's—we have plenty of time, sit down, take off your coat, stay a while—(*She doesn't.*) Oh, Nan! I saw Pip on his *show*! Have you seen his—

Nan No.

Walker It was the first day I was back—

Nan And what day was that?

Walker I passed this store, there was this bank of television sets, all tuned to *Pip*—I went in—I insisted they turn up the volume—it was extraordinary. He plays someone named *Butte* who never wears a shirt and is carnally entangled with someone named *Savannah*—they must have met during an earthquake—anyway, he's all sort of rough and tender and monosyllabic and you'd never guess his father was a dead legend—

8

Nan Well, don't torture him about it.

Walker I . . . don't—

Nan Listen. Look. We'd better allow plenty of time for traffic—

Walker The appointment's not for—

Nan If you get snarled up in—

Walker It's three minutes by *rick*shaw, we won't—

Nan You come late for these estate lawyers and they penalize you in acreage—

Walker Oh God, I haven't seen you in a year and all you can talk about is itinerary—would you please please please just for a second drop this goddamned suburban alacrity and *hug* me? (*He hugs her. She barely submits. Then holds him tight. Then moves out of it.*)

Nan And just for the record: I do not live in the suburbs—I live in the city.

Walker (*Appalled.*) You live in *Boston*.

Nan Boston is a city.

Walker Boston is not a city, Boston is a *parish*.

Nan Oh, please.

Walker What could ever possibly happen to you on a street in Boston? You might, what, run into a *cleric* and *repent* something? Boston is only a city if you're a swan boat. You're supposed to realize that.

Nan Yes, I know: Boston is not a city, Detroit is not a city, Chicago is merely the exception that proves the rule about the Midwest—

Walker All that is true.

9

Nan I don't hold by any of it anymore, you know.

Walker (*Oddly serious.*) I sincerely hope that's not true. . . . Your life has made you so—

Nan You haven't even asked me one thing about my life since I—

Walker Yes. You're absolutely right. I'm sorry. How are you? How's Harry? How are the twins? They must be . . . different shapes, by now.

Nan . . . Nick has started to read.

Walker That's great.

Nan And Milly is ice skating like a—

Walker (*Overlaps.*) Oh, terrific.

Nan They're really spectacular.
   They're not twins, of course, but that's the sort of detail I don't expect you to have memorized.

Walker I know that, I—oh, look all children to me are, you know me and—they're all more or less one child taken to some unfathomable power, one *überkind,* all noisy and candid and tormenting, why don't you *sit*?

Nan *I don't* want *to sit!* (*Pause.*)

Walker . . . Nan?

Nan I thought you were dead this time.

Walker I, yes, you—

Nan I was certain of it, this time—

Walker I'm—

Nan There were things to think of at the funeral other than your absence, Walker. Did you ever consider us for a moment in this last year? Do you have any idea what it was like?

Harry hired detectives. It cost us a fortune. We learned *nothing*. For such a fuck-up you're incredibly gifted at getting lost. *Where were you?*

Walker Italy. (*Beat.*)

Nan Italy?

Walker Yes.

Nan Just . . . Italy?

Walker Yes, I know, anything short of Jupiter must sound prosaic after all you've been through, but—one town in particular for most of it. Well, eventually. In Tuscany.

Nan God!

Walker Um, I know, it's the most obvious possible pla—those detectives must have been quite second-rate; anyway, well, I'd been told nobody goes there anymore—an enormous lie, by the way—so I decided to try it out.
   Oh, I had this memory—I think it was from a movie—of a field of bachelor's buttons and tall trees. I rented this very cheap but quite fine villa for a while—to study it, you know. I wanted to learn the bones of the building, I thought maybe I'd end up writing something. I spent months pretending I was that sort of person made ecstatic by olive oil, do you know? I very nearly *was,* for a bit. But nothing came of any of it.

Nan You just . . . walked out of your apartment; you abandoned—

Walker It had become—the filth of it—the chaos of it—it just happened. So I left. And *I did* go to the cemetery. The morning after the . . . event. Three o'clock or something.

Nan Jesus.

Walker It's nice where Ned is, isn't it? Under that tree, right by the water. He has a belvedere. I just sort of showed up with my rucksack. I'd brought—oh God, you're not hearing this from me—I'd brought a candle. I'd decided to have a private ceremony. Luckily, it was raining, the candle, the wick wouldn't light. So I just sat on that big boulder by his grave, getting wet and chatting away like a moron. The dead man said nothing. So like the living.

Then, away.

Now here. Home to you.

Nan I could strangle you with my bare hands.

Walker Okay. . . .

Were they nice? The obsequies, I mean?

Nan They were . . . big.

Walker (*Laughs a little.*) Yes.

Nan Very big.

Walker A *do*! And I missed it.

Nan It was filled with personages. The Finnish ambassador. Did he build something in Finland? The lieutenant governor—Kitty Carlisle!

Walker Hart.

Nan I forget sometimes . . . what he was, the scope of the life he'd made. The whole city turned out—

Walker And "mother"—was she—?

Nan No.

I wasn't permitted to tell her for, I think, two months. She didn't know he was dead for two months.

Or that you were missing.

Or her *name* half the time, probab—finally, they thought they'd found the right cocktail of drugs, it seems they'd brought her to equilibrium. I went there. Lina seemed fine. Truly. She was funny about her "recovery." She said: "Look

at me—all this nonsense because of jumbled hormones—and when I was young we thought it was an excess of *soul*."
Really: more Tallulah than ever. It's hard to connect that with Sanity Regained, but. . . . So I told her.

Walker And did she—

Nan Relapsed a couple of days later.
   You haven't spoken to her in, what, five years?

Walker Three, *two*—

Nan You ought to. On a good day, she's exactly like you, only old.
   . . . You're not planning on disappearing again any time soon, are you?

Walker Not planning it.

Nan Thank you.
   But you're not living *here*. What *is* this place anyway? How did you find it?

Walker It was theirs.

Nan "Theirs." Whose?

Walker Ned's and Theo's. (*Beat.*)

Nan What do you—when?

Walker 1960. Right at the beginning.
   I came back to town. All I had were my coat and a bag and about a billion traveler's checks—

Nan When did you have time to get traveler's—

Walker Most of my money is *in* traveler's checks. Anyway, I wandered around for a while. I stayed one night at this Catholic hotel on Twenty-Third Street, then—I forget. Then I remembered Lawyer Fisher. He told me about this. He gave me the keys. They lived here thirty-five years ago. They were roommates, did you know that? That's the only thing I could find resembling a mattress. Do you suppose they were—

Nan Walker—God—

Walker It's possible—

Nan Not everyone is as sexually fluent as you, Walker—our loss, perhaps, but the *case*—he *kept* this?

Walker All this time. Intact, as far as I can make out. It was a rental at the start. He purchased it at some point, the whole building, I suppose it's ours now—very Grand Ducal, don't you—oh! I found a picture from early on—that gallery across the street—(*Crosses to window.*)

Nan It's not a gallery—

Walker It was an Italian restaurant then—for some reason they're still—I got coffee there, the gallery serves—

Nan It's still some kind of restaurant; they've just added art.

Walker I can't tell what it is. They gave me a cigar! The building's the same, though—Ned and Lina must have eaten there, don't you think? With the red-checkered breadsticks and melting Chianti bot—oh! And the two stores next to it were one building and maybe empty—there's the most wonderful *bricolage* —all this stuff covering old stuff and old stuff that's been scraped away to reveal older stuff—Look! (*Turning back inside.*)
   The drafting table!
   This must have been Ned's and Theo's studio, too. They must have designed the house here, don't you think? This must have been the hovel they were living in when they laid the plans for that paradise—

Nan Walker, we shouldn't be here—

Walker It's *ours*!
   Nan, it was the weirdest feeling, walking in the first time.

The place is so nothing. I couldn't imagine why he'd kept it. I paced the floor for two days, screaming at the walls: "Speak! Speak!" It was infuriating.

Nan We should go somewhere—you need to eat—

Walker This place made as little sense as anything else. Finally, last night, I couldn't sleep, I felt something against my back, under the mattress, no, it *was* "The Princess and the Pea," I rolled off the bed, reached under and found *this:* (*He extracts a notebook.*)

It's a kind of diary, a journal. The inevitable journal! I think that's why he kept this place, it's The House of the Journal. I've been poring over it, my brain's all ragged, I can't make head or tale of it, but it seems to cover *everything:* when they built the house, everybody getting married, births, institutionalizations, etcetera—it *seems* to—it's practically written in cipher. And there are whole bunches of years covered by a single sentence. Still. (*Nan is staring at the journal.*) I know. It gives off an infernal *glow,* doesn't it?

Nan Put it away.

Walker You're cracked.

Nan Put it away now.

Walker We have to read this together, Nan; it insists.

Nan Walker—

Walker (*Firm.*) We *are* reading this today.
I've been away but now I'm back.
We're going to read this and then we're going to the lawyer's and receive what's been left us.
What we should have had a year ago, but for me.
This is the day, Nan.
We're finally going to find out what belongs to us.
(*Lights.*)

Nan (*Solo.*) Plans for the building that would come to be known as Janeway House were completed sometime in the fall of 1960. Ground was broken in early spring of the following year, and my grandparents moved into their new home that winter.

The house was begun modestly, but became instantly famous when it was chosen for the cover of one of the tonier architectural quarterlies of the day—

Walker It became famous when the picture was published in *LIFE*—

Nan It was published first in—

Walker But it only became *famous* when it was published in *LIFE*—

Nan Either way.

I never learned, quite, the technical reasons that the house is great—my brother is better on those, Walker has actually studied that stuff—

Walker I'm not going to go into it—

Nan —but it has something to do with fenestration—

Walker Not really—

Nan —and the solids and the, the alternation of solids and—

Walker (*Overlapping.*)—*voids*—the solids and the voids—

Nan And there's a kind of miracle about the light—

Walker All the glass, the house is a prism, but you don't broil in it in the summer—

Nan —and there's a different kind of light in every room, and at every hour—and the rooms themselves have something liquid about them, something that changes. Goethe—Goethe was it?

Walker Some famous German—

Nan —defined architecture as "frozen music."

Walker This is the quality the plans don't capture—

Nan According to the monograph writers, when you look at them, they're very fine, but they somehow don't imply the house itself. Apparently, that's how it is sometimes with great buildings—

Walker There's an intuition held in reserve, a secret the architect keeps until the building is built. It may only be that the plans actually work.

Nan It's also said that of the great houses of the last forty years, this is the best one for living in. . . .

My parents married because it was 1960 and one had to and they were there. And I don't think that's a contemptible thing—for people who have reached a certain age and never found anything better.

I mean, forget about what happened later, think of the *moment*. My mother was lovely, but not as young as she should have been, my father was virtually silent, and they *found* each other and I don't think that's so cynical. He was presentable and serious and he must have seemed calming to her, and solid, and easy to ignore, but not in a bad way. And he was from New England and later New York, so he probably thought she wasn't crazy, just Southern. And if it was calculating, it was a calculation against loneliness, against . . . the possibility of no life at all.

On May 12th, 1972, at around eight P.M., I was in the kitchen of our eleven-room apartment on the Upper East Side, finishing up the dishes and humming. We were living then in a terrible skyscraper my father had designed, his first skyscraper—

Walker —his first building after Theo died—

Nan My brother, who was eight, was in his pajamas, on the living room floor, erecting cities out of this super-sophisticated Tinker Toy kind of thing my father had made for us. My father sat in a large, uncomfortable Modern chair, flipping silently through an art book—

Walker We had dined *à trois* that night because at around seven, my mother had stationed herself in the middle of the long foyer, and for the hour since had been rocking on her haunches, muttering in a private language of her own invention.

Nan I had done with the dishes and was moving onto the water glasses when something happened. The first indication I had was the sound of my brother laughing. He later told me he hadn't reacted to anything new, he'd just looked up and in an instant really seen what was happening—

Walker And I lost it. I mean, it was uncontrollable. Anyway, this triggered something in my mother so she just dashed out of there. She flew out the apartment and down the thousands of flights of stairs all the way to the lobby.

Nan My brother pursued her but couldn't catch her—

Walker There was, I'm sure, an amphetamine involved—

Nan He did arrive in time however to see her body pierce the glass facade of the building—

Walker It was incredible! Straight through. There was this moment, before the blood started, when she looked like something crystal. Then *bam!*—colorized—this sudden redness—everywhere—

Nan My brother was eight years old.
   Meanwhile, upstairs, my father, acting on a hunch, instructed me to telephone for an ambulance while he joined in the chase. I called the ambulance, dried the glasses from

dinner, and sat on the long, steep, uncomfortable couch. Waiting. I was ten.

Sometimes, I ask people, "So how did all of this happen?" and they say, "Oh well, your poor mother, you know, and then, it *was* the sixties."

At any rate.

My mother was taken to the hospital where they did very good work. My brother ran away, but only as far as the laundry room of our building, where he hid in a closet for ten hours until someone thought to check there. My brother returned, my mother returned. Nobody said anything. And it was over.

(*Lights.*)

Walker (*Reading from journal.*) "May 12, 1972: A terrible night."

Nan Walker, stop.

Walker No—I am *not* making this up:
"May 12, 1972: A terrible night."
That evening—

Nan Yes—

Walker This is the only sentence he devotes to it. In my delirium, I thought maybe a page was missing, but no, the subsequent entry is right in place: "May 13, 1972: Food at New York Hospital surprisingly edible."

Nan Please—

Walker I mean, it really is the most extraordinary document. The first thing you notice when you start reading is the style: It doesn't have one. And it manages to sustain that for hundreds of pages—you flip through—narratives of the most wrenching events, and the affect is entirely flat—wait—listen to this—winter of 1966—you know, when Theo is going under?

19

Listen to our father's rendering:

"January 3—Theo is dying."

"January 5—Theo is dying."

"January 18"—(I'll skip a little)—"Theo dead."

I mean! His partner. Best and oldest friend: "Theo dying, Theo dying, Theo dead." You could sing it to the tune of "Ob-La-Di."

And it's all like that. Every entry. Years and years of—wait—this is the best of all—the first note—the kickoff, you'll—listen:

"1960, April 3rd to April 5th—Three days of rain." (*Beat.*) Okay. Look. Let's—

Reconstruct along with me a moment. You are this young man. Ambitious, of course—what architect isn't ambitious? And it's that moment when you're so bursting with feeling that people aren't enough, your art isn't enough, you need something else, some other way to let out everything that's in you. You buy this notebook, this volume into which you can pour your most secret, your deepest and illicit passions. You bring it home, commence—the first sacred jottings—the feelings you couldn't contain:

"April 3rd to April 5th: Three days of rain." A weather report. *A fucking weather report!* (*Beat. He quiets down.*)

You know, the thing is with people who never talk, the thing is you always suppose they're harboring some enormous secret. But, just possibly, the secret is, they have *absolutely nothing to say.* (*Beat.*)

Anyway, I want you to give me the house.

Nan What?

Walker I want the house. I want to buy your share in—

Nan Why?

Walker I just—need to—

Nan You hated him. Why do you want his house?

20

Walker Because I don't live anywhere.

Oh, look, look, I can't be sure of this but I think when I got lost this last time, when I disappeared, it was so that you would find me. I know that makes me an impossible person, I *am* an impossible person, it's fact, but, anyway, when all those months passed and no one showed up, I started to believe you had forgotten me. I don't mean as in "ceased to care," I mean as in, "couldn't place the name." That's absurd, but I was living in a country where I didn't speak the language and it started to seem truly possible. Crazy—but that's not exactly foreign terrain for us, is it? I really started to believe I was going—crazy, I—

Nan (*Softly.*) Sweetie—

Walker The reason I don't like being around people who are like me only old is that they always seem to be ending so badly. I don't want to end badly. And I don't want to be this burden on people I love so much. And the house is very beautiful. I think it could only have been designed by someone who was happy. And I'd like to believe that was part of it, too. I love the city, but it's dangerous to me. It's let me . . . become nothing.

I want to be sane. I want a place that belongs to me.
Let me have the house. Please. (*Beat.*)

Nan Put away the book.

Walker . . . But—

Nan Put away the book and never take it out again. The house for the book. That's my offer. (*A hesitation. Walker replaces the journal beneath the mattress.*) And that's the end of it.

Walker Yes. Thank you.

Nan Now let's go or we really will be late.

Walker Yes, yes . . . let me get my coat.

Nan I'll wait outside. (*She goes out. Walker puts on his coat, retrieves the book, buries it in a pocket, joins her outside.*) You're ready?

Walker Absolutely.
 Nan. You'll come all the time, won't you? It'll be everyone . . .

Nan Of course. Let's go. We don't want to leave Pip alone with the lawyer.

Walker God, no—he might try to work out a side deal! (*They leave. Lights.*)

> (*The sound of car brakes squealing. Pip rushes on, as though late, slams door behind him, catches his breath, smiles at audience.*)

Pip (*Solo.*) Hi. Hello. Okay: now me.
 My name is Phillip O'Malley Wexler—well, Pip to those who've known me a little too long. My father, the architect Theodore Wexler, died of lung cancer at the age of thirty-eight, even though he was the only one of his generation who never smoked. I was three when it happened, so, of course, I forgot him instantly. My mother tried to make up for this by obsessively telling me stories about him, this kind of rolling epic that trailed me through life, but they, or *it,* ended up being mostly about her. Which was probably for the best.
 Anyway, it went like this:
 My mother, Maureen O'Malley back then, came to New York in the spring of '59. She was twenty, her parents staked her to a year, and she arrived with a carefully-thought-out plan to be amazing at something. Well, the year went by without much happening and she was miserable because she was afraid she was going to have to leave New York and return, in disgrace, to Brooklyn.
 Early one morning, after a night when she couldn't sleep at all, she started wandering around the city. It was raining, she

had her umbrella, she sat in the rain under her umbrella on a bench in Washington Square Park, and felt sorry for herself. Then she saw my father for the first time.

"There he was," she told me, "this devastatingly handsome man"—that was an exaggeration, he looked like me—and he was obviously, miraculously, even *more* unhappy than she was. He was just thrashing through the rain, pacing and thrashing, until, all at once, he stopped and sank onto the bench beside her. But not because of her. He didn't realize she was there. He didn't have an umbrella so my mother shifted hers over to him.

"Despair," my mother told me, "can be attractive in a young person. Despair in a young person can be seductive."

Well, eventually she got tired of him not noticing the wonderful thing she was doing for him so she said, a little too loudly:

"Can I help you? May I be of help to you?"

Because he'd been crying.

And he jumped! Man, he *shrieked*!

But he stayed anyway, and they talked, and I was born, the end.

Okay. So, my mother had been telling me that story for about ten years before it occurred to me to ask: "Why was he crying? What was my father so upset about the first time he met you?" "I never knew," she said. He just told her he was fine, she took him to breakfast, they talked about nothing, and I guess she kind of gawked at him. And the more she gawked, I guess the happier he felt, because by the end of breakfast it was as if nothing had happened and they were laughing and my mother was in love and the worst day of her life had become the best day of her life.

When she first came to New York, my mother would stay up till dawn debating Abstract Expressionism and *Krapp's Last Tape,* and then she'd sneak out to a matinee of one of those plays you could never remember the plot of where the girl got caught in the rain and had to put on the man's bathrobe and they sort of did a little dance around each other and fell in love. And there wasn't even a single good joke, but my mother would walk out after and the city seemed dizzy with this absolutely random happiness, and that's how she met my father.

She's hardly ever home anymore. She travels from city to city.

I think she's looking for another park bench, and another wet guy. That's okay. I hope she finds him. (*Lights. Walker sits outside the apartment building. Nan and Pip are inside. Nan is seated in the window, quite still. Pip paces.*)

Nan I know, Pip.

Pip I mean, it's incredible, I mean, I can't believe it!

Nan I know that, yes—

Pip It's the same thing all over again—it's the same thing, Nan—

Nan I know—

Pip I mean, when Walker was gone, all I could remember was all the great things about him. Which when you think about it is a pretty meager amount of material to spread out over a year—

Nan I—yes—

Pip Well, I mean, no, not really, but this stuff, this stuff! I mean, you'd think returning from the dead would be character-improving, but I mean: Look at him. He *chooses* to *sit* there in the pretty cold *evening*, and, somehow, *I* feel guilty about it! As if I were the weather! Or something. I mean—

Nan Yes—

Pip What he said to me, Jesus, at the *lawyer's*! He's *my* lawyer, too, you know. Can you imagine how *chagrined* I'll be next time I have to—okay, not that I ever really need to use him, so it's not that bad, I guess—but still to be the victim of this—Shakespearean tirade—or at least Maxwell Anderson—as if I'd *done* something—which I haven't—but still I feel guilty about it because he's in *so much pain*. You know?

Nan Yes, I—

Pip And I'm really hungry—I haven't eaten anything but star fruit all day—but we have to wait while he *sits*—in the cold for which I am responsible—for him to gather his wits and tell us it's all right to eat. And I feel *bad* because he's in *so much pain*—

Nan Yes—

Pip I mean, it was a terrible thing—I guess—what happened there—

Nan It was—

Pip It was a brutal thing—in a way—and I feel awful about it—but it's something that a dead man—may he rest in peace, God rest his soul—did—and I'm sorry to refer to your father that way but—

Nan "Dead man" is all right—

Pip —but I didn't do it. And Walker is great, I mean, don't get me wrong, Walker is great. He's great. Sometimes I *question* Walker's greatness, but he's great . . . and he's in *so much pain*—but to *call me* things like that in front of all the wood and the leather and the lawyer—it's really inexcusable, it's incorrigible. And you can't say anything to him. You can't scream at him, you can't disapprove of him, you can't even, you know, mildly *remonstrate* with him because he's in *so much pain*.

Nan Yes.

Pip I mean, has there ever been a time when he wasn't in *so much pain*?

Nan No.

Pip No, I mean, I remember when we were *ten,* not doing things because he was in *so much pain.* I connected everything to it: "I better not eat that baloney sandwich, Walker is in *so much pain.*" I mean, a ten-year-old boy shouldn't be so emotionally, whatever, *fastidious* about another ten-year-old boy's feelings, but, with *him.* . .

Nan I know.

Pip There comes a time, Nan, there just comes a point when you have to say: Enough, I don't care that you're in so much pain, you cannot behave like this any longer. (*Beat.*) But you can't because he's in *so much pain.*

Nan I know.

Pip I didn't do anything like what he accused me of, Nan, I didn't manipulate anything; you believe that, don't you?

Nan Can we talk about something else?

Pip Shit.

Nan How are you, or something? We haven't had a chance to—

Pip Nan.

Nan Oh look, we're *stuck* here, you know, we're—and I haven't spoken to you in too long and I've *missed you,* so can't we just . . . how *are* you? (*Beat.*) Please. (*Beat. Pip takes a breath, relaxes, smiles.*)

Pip Well . . . you know . . . I'm great, mostly. Mostly I'm great.

Nan I'm glad. . . . And Maureen?

Pip Mom's doing good, thank you. She sends a big hello from Prague, by the way. And your mother? (*Nan raises an eye-*

brow.) Sorry. (*Nan looks at him, starts to smile*.) What . . . what?

Nan I watch you on that show.

Pip That's mortifying.

Nan When I don't have anything in the afternoon. There you are . . . shirtlessly . . . doing things.

Pip Are you ashamed of me?

Nan Ashamed?

Pip When you watch, does it make you—

Nan It makes me smile, to see you.

Pip That's what I'll think of tomorrow, when I'm taping.

Nan You enjoy it, don't you?

Pip I do, I really do. I mean, I really do. People recognize me. Well, "Butte," anyway. And they treat me well, they *give* me things—because of this ridiculous part, it's wild!

Nan I can't imagine it's much of a *chal*lenge though.

Pip Well, you know, I think for a really *great* actor it wouldn't be? But for me it sort of is?

Nan You're a very good actor.

Pip No, I'm not.

Nan You *are*—that thing you did we saw that time, that was very—

Pip No, no it's okay. I don't need to be some great actor. That just makes it even more magical somehow, you know that I'm doing so well when I'm really so *eh*. I don't need bucking up. I see these other people on the show in their dressing rooms with their little Signet editions of *Pericles, Prince of Tyre*, or whatever, *studying*. And it's so pathetic.

27

These people shouldn't be studying, they should be *investing*. But you can't say anything to them because they're Persons of the Theatre, they go to *class*. I'm so lucky! I can't believe it! I get to go to great restaurants, I pick up the check, pretty girls will date me, I eat chocolate and never gain weight, life is *good* . . .

Nan Good.

Pip And you? I mean, other than the obvious?

Nan . . . Yes, fine. No, lovely, truly.

Pip Milly must, be, like, four-and-a-half now?

Nan Yes. Exactly.

Pip And Nick, I know, last-week-I-sent-the-toy, he's just three.

Nan Yes. They're fantastic.

Pip That's great. And Harry?

Nan He's—

Pip He's the best person.

Nan Well, he's—

Pip I'm sorry, unless you can't stand him anymore or something, in which case: *feh*.

Nan No. He *is* the best person.

Pip I always thought that. Does he still have his hair?

Nan . . . Yes.

Pip That, too!

Nan Uh-huh. He's quite amazing.
    He always says the right thing.

Pip . . . Okay.

Nan No, I don't mean it like that, I don't mean the socially *graceful* thing—sometimes he will say the very opposite of the—that can be *harrowing* when that happens but . . . he's just so *kind,* do you know?
   So unbelievably . . . (*She looks at Pip.*)
   He's what *you* would be if—

Pip If I had substance?

Nan If I hadn't met you till I was twenty-five.

Pip Then when you think of me, it's not with unbridled scorn?

Nan Not unbridled.

Pip Mingled with affection?

Nan *You,* Phillip, are my role model.

Pip (*Smiles, a bit shy.*) Thank you.
   Listen, I'm just going, I'm starving, I'm gonna get something at that new cigar bar across the street—I think I read they serve food; so what if I have to walk past him? Can I get you something? Or will you come or—

Nan I'll wait.

Pip I'll be back in a— (*Heading out, Pip bumps into Walker, who's heading in.*) Oh. Hey.

Walker Hello. (*Silence. They all arrange themselves in the room.*)

Pip I was just—do you want to go get food?

Walker I'm not actually hungry. If you are, you can—

Pip No, that's fine, I'm fine. (*Beat. Silence. Walker looks to Nan.*)

Walker I'm very sorry, Pip. What I said to you at the lawyers was really, really awful.

29

Pip Wow.

Walker It's just, you see, when the thing happened . . . it was unbearable.

Pip Oh sure, I mean, yeah.

Walker (*Overlapping.*) It was really excruciating and—

Pip Well, it must have been—

Walker And I, typically made it into this vast, sort of Oedipal saga, totally over the top—

Pip (*Overlapping from "over the top."*) Which is a story that doesn't even make sense when you think about it, but no, Walker, this is really terrific—

Walker (*Overlapping.*) and I realize that I was wrong—what?

Pip What?

Walker *What* doesn't make sense?

Pip What? Oh, nothing.

Walker You said something doesn't—

Pip No, I, no. I just want to thank you for apologizing. I know that's not easy for you and—

Nan "Oedipus" doesn't make sense?

Walker That *is* what he said. In what way doesn't "Oedipus" make sense?

Pip Oh, no, I, that was, I don't want to get into it. (*But they're staring at him.*) No, I mean, just from a practical point of view, not in any deep-structural way or . . . anything. (*Beat.*) No, I mean, it's just, like . . . if some oracle told you you were going to kill your father and marry your mother, wouldn't you just never kill anybody and stay single? . . . And then, if you *did* inadvertently kill somebody, in the heat of the moment or something, and later started dating? Wouldn't you be smart enough to, like, *avoid older women*? I mean, to me the moral of that story is not your destiny awaits you. To me it's . . . you know . . . Do the Fucking Math. (*Beat.*)

Walker You must publish.

Pip Walker.

Walker It would be a crime if these insights were limited to this room.

Pip Okay, Walker, I wasn't pretending—

Walker No: Really, we must notify the university presses at once to—

Nan Walker.

Walker Yes, I meant not to do that.

Pip I walked right into—

Walker You did.

Nan You always do.

Pip I do. I always do. Walker, let me just say it—

Nan Can we go somewhere, can we eat something?

Pip What happened at the lawyer's, doesn't mean your father hated you.

Walker Uumm . . . was that proposed?

Pip I don't know why I got the house.

Walker I don't think I ever said—God! "Hate"—I mean—!

Pip I know that's what has to be going through your head.

Walker Well now it is.

31

Pip But I'm sure it wasn't that—it wasn't even necessarily insensitive, you know.

Nan (*Involuntary.*) It was wicked. (*A hesitation.*) I said nothing.

Pip You know, it's not as if he disinherited you. You got a fortune, literally a fortune.

Walker That's beside the point.

Pip No, wait, no, that can't be, I mean, there is no point so *huge* that that much money can be *beside* it.

Walker I would have traded it for the house.

Pip That would have been *dumb*.

Walker Oh, Christ.

Pip Look I'm just caught up in this, I'm not the mastermind behind it, I don't even know how it's possible, really, I mean, why didn't it revert to your mom?

Nan He got it in the divorce.

Pip In the divorce?

Nan Yes.

Pip They were divorced?

Nan Oh God.

Pip How did I miss that?

Walker You have your ways.

Nan We were in college. They'd been separated so long by then, it was practically just paperwork. Anyway, it didn't change anything.

Pip I can't believe I—

Nan It doesn't matter.

Pip Anyway, the point is, Walker, you were wrong.

Walker I've already apologized.

Pip Not just wrong to say it: incorrect. Your dad and I—it was not some sort of quasi-paternal "substitution" or "alienation of affection" or whatever you called it. You know what your dad was to me: this nice kind of uncle, I wasn't *working on* him or—

Walker I realize that.

Pip I'd just drop by occasionally, in the afternoons, if I had an audition in the neighborhood or something. It wasn't any big deal.

Walker Yes, I know.

Pip I was just somebody he found it easy to talk to. (*Sudden frigid silence.*)

Walker Ah.

Pip He was a pretty lonely man in the last few years. I don't think he was doing that much work on his own, all the partners were always buzzing around, he'd be twiddling his thumbs. I'd just pop in. I thought it was my responsibility. You were in Boston. *You* were always flittering off to Peru or Rhode Island or wherever. We'd sit and gab.

Walker And what would you "gab" about?

Pip We'd—whatever was going on—sports!

Walker . . . Sports?

Pip Or anything. Don't ask me for details, they weren't colloquies, it was just chat—easy, you know?

Walker . . . I see.

Pip And I never made a single overture about the house. I, the ironic part is, I can't even use the house, really; frankly, I don't even like it much.

Walker You don't *like* it much?

Pip No.

Walker That's not acceptable.

Pip It's just my opinion.

Walker You don't get to have an opinion.

Pip I got the *house*. I think I should be allowed to express a point of view—

Walker That doesn't follow.

Pip Look, it's not that I think it's *bad* work, I just find it a little stark.

Walker Stark.

Pip Yes.

Walker Stark!

Pip Yes!

Walker Well, what do you know? Before you favored us with your views on Greek Tragedy, and now we get to hear you hold forth on Architecture as well. I never before realized you were a cultural critic of such extreme *scope*—

Pip Don't start.

Walker No, no, I want *more*, I want to hear you on, you know, Hegel and Umberto Eco—Boolean Algebra—

Pip Walker, stop.

Walker No, it's such a privilege to learn what a TV actor who plays a character named after a geological formation has to *say* about the really important events in world culture—

Nan Walker—

Walker I'm especially interested in your visual aesthetic—

Nan Please be quiet.

Walker Because I think the real innovations are going to come from people who buy antiqued Italianate chiffarobes from catalogues.

Pip You're not exactly one to comment on anyone's environment, Walker.

Walker Oh, really?

Pip After where you were living, that apartment.

Walker That—?

Pip I mean, really: interior decoration by Jeffrey Dahmer.

Walker You saw where I was—

Pip I was your "in case of emergency" contact. So don't get hoity-toity about it. I swear, it was horrible, it was crazy, I thought it was your mom all over again.

Walker We would love you to be silent, now.

Pip I mean, why do you get to be the one who judges things when you're having the stupidest life of anybody? I'm sick of it, Walker. *You're* the one who's done the bad thing here, you're the one who ran off like a maniac and left us to go bonkers worrying about you. I've been good, Nan's been good, you've been bad. Okay, that's the morality of the situation. So you don't get to make the laws; that's the upshot.

Walker I wish—

Pip No, *I'm* talking now, and it's a very weird sensation. Look, Walker, look—it's just you can't be the only personality in the room anymore. You cannot just change the temperature of every circumstance by this kind of tyrannical psychosocial, you know, *fiat*—oh, *look,* I know you think I'm an idiot—

Walker I never said you were an idiot.

Pip Yes, you did, you said it all the time, you just pretended sometimes not to mean it; but I know you meant it.

Walker I didn't.

Pip Even though *I* was the one who was off the charts in any standardized exam we ever took, while you were always getting *lost* on the way to the *test*ing center. But that doesn't matter, I know—with your exquisite perversity that just *proves* it, but look, the fact is, it isn't true—being in a good mood is not the same thing as being a moron. It just isn't. And, you know, for years I wondered. I strove to sustain some level of unhappiness because I felt so left out but I couldn't manage it—

Walker I never intended you to—

Pip I don't know—I feel bad—I go to the gym—I feel better. Maybe that means I lack *gravitas* or something, but the hell with it, I'm having a good time.

Walker I'm glad for—

Pip Except I am no longer willing to bear the brunt of your *mean*ness.

Walker I'm sorry, I—

Pip You know, it's not as if I don't know where it's coming from, it's not as if I don't know you've always been basically in love with me—that's been so obvious for so many years that—

Walker Oh Jesus—Jesus—

Pip I don't know what—but why does it have to be such a problem? Why couldn't we have just worked it through when we were eighteen? It would have been so easy. I would have been sensitive, you would have suffered for a while, it would have been over, and we could have spent the next fifteen years going to the movies or something like *people*. Instead of it fucking up everything.

Walker This is a little too—

Pip Because it's just fucked up everything for such a long time—everything we had to keep from you—

Nan Pip.

Pip . . . the stupid, gothic secrets—the tiptoeing around—

Nan Pip.

Pip I mean, like all that time when Nan and I were sleeping together and in love and everything and we couldn't tell you because we were so afraid of how jealous you'd be, and we couldn't tell each other why we couldn't tell you because nobody was acknowledging any aspect of the situation—it was crazy, that felt awful—I hated lying to you. Like it or not, you're my oldest friend. I love you, you know, and what was the point? Everything is tolerable if you just *talk* about it, you know? (*Beat. Silence between Walker and Nan.*) You know? (*Beat.*) Was that *all* new information?

Walker I'm going to get something to eat at the place. Don't come there, okay? (*He exits.*)

Pip Oh. Oh damn. I had no idea. That was such a long time ago, I assumed—do things really stay secret that long? (*Beat.*) Nan?

Nan Well, it's a stupid thing. It's just a stupid thing.

Pip It's nothing at this point, isn't it? We were, like, eighteen years old, even *his* statute of limitations must have run out by now. This won't be a big deal.

Nan It will go on forever. (*Beat. Looks at her watch.*) I'm not going to make it home to put my kids to bed.

Pip If you catch the next shuttle—

Nan I won't catch the next shuttle. (*Pause.*) What was hard when he finally called, what was hard was to realize he was still alive. For the first . . . nine months, I think, every day I woke up in a panic—if I'd slept—with these unbearably vivid pictures of what had befallen him. And I'd go through most of the day mourning. Then it would occur to me that what I was so certain had happened to him almost certainly had not happened to him—the mere fact of my inventing it had made it unlikely—and there would be a momentary, I don't know, *rest,* I suppose. And I'd go on to imagine some other horrible thing. Then . . . it stopped. I don't know how. I realized it afterward—some *weeks* afterward—I was on to other things. I was back . . . with my children. I was back in the day. At home. In Boston. And it was sad, but better. It was much better.

What I mean is, when I heard his voice the main feeling was not relief. (*Pause.*)

Today, when he asked for the house, I thought, oh God, yes, take the house, let him have it, the house will take care of him. And I'll be free. (*Beat.*) Do you want to get something to eat? I've got a lot of time to kill.

Pip I'll give him the house.

Nan You can't do that.

Pip Why not? It's mine, I can do whatever I want with it.

Nan You can't do that for him.

Pip Well, in the first place I'm doing it for you—

Nan God, that's—

Pip . . . and, second, I don't even really want it and he needs it, and I, well, really can't stand to think of you unhappy, and I've got the solution so—hey: Christmas!

Nan You cannot *give* it away. Do you have any idea how much that house is worth?

Pip Okay, then I'll sell it to him; that's even better.

Nan But—

Pip He can afford it after all the money he got—you, too! Good God, am I the only one who realizes this was a *good day*?

Nan Do you *mean* this?

Pip Yes!

Nan Can I go tell him now?

Pip Yes.

Nan I will.

Pip And then I'll take you to the airport.

Nan I—what?

Pip If we leave in ten minutes, you can make the plane.

Nan . . . Pip.

Pip That's my stipulation.

Nan I—

Pip Or the deal is off.

Nan But—

Pip I will sell him the house, but you have to go home.

Nan You are . . . (*She can't find the word for his wonderfulness.*)

Pip (*Accepting the compliment.*) Yes, I am. Go! (*Nan heads out. Pip stays behind a moment. Looks at the room. He touches the surface of the drafting table. Something like a shudder goes through him. Nan reenters.*)

Nan He's gone.

Pip ... Are you—? Did you look every—?

Nan It's a tiny place—he's gone off.

Pip We can get a cab at the corner.

Nan I can't get on that plane without even—he's God-knows-where—

Pip It doesn't make a difference.

Nan Pip—

Pip You can pretend he's dead. (*Beat.*) He's dead, Nan. (*Long pause.*)

Nan Let me have a minute.

Pip I'll get the cab. (*Pip heads outside. She looks around, indecisive. She lifts up the mattress. There's nothing underneath it.*)

Nan God*damn* him! (*Blackout.*)

(*Late that night. The apartment is dark. Walker enters. Nan is in darkness, curled up on the mattress.*)

Nan Hello...

Walker Oh, Jesus! (*He flips on the lights.*) You're still here.

Nan I fell asleep.

Walker I figured you'd gone.

Nan Oh. I almost did. I *should* have. I didn't.

Walker I'm glad.

Nan I turned around at the last minute. I almost made it to the bridge.

Walker Pip—?

Nan ... went home.

Walker Ah. (*Beat.*)

Nan Where did you go?

Walker I was—every corner of this city—it was—I . . . couldn't stop moving. I tried to calm myself. I . . . got coffee at a couple of—that was a bad idea—I ended up counting the Wexler Janeway buildings I passed; that was no help at all. I stopped at fourteen.

Nan Fourteen! You must have been to Brooklyn.

Walker I was to—Staten Island!

Nan Jesus.

Walker Not very young, not very merry, but I rode back and forth for hours on the—

Nan What time is it, anyway?

Walker I have no idea; did you ever eat?

Nan No.

Walker (*Burrowing in his rucksack, pulling out a paper bag.*) I've got—I picked up this stuff from a deli tray. It's probably still all right. (*Opens the bag.*)

Nan What is it?

Walker I think either tiramisu . . . or squid.

Nan I pass. (*Beat.*)

Walker Thank you for staying. (*She nods.*) So . . . we don't have to talk about it.

Nan Thank *you*.

Walker . . . So how long did it go on?

Nan Walker—

Walker Was it *fun*, was he *good*, what—

Nan I don't want to discuss it.

Walker Okay.

Nan I'm sorry that I kept it from you all this time.

Walker No, that's all right. Actually, it feels quite invigorating to be apologized *to* for a change, that doesn't happen very oft—*tell me,* at least, did it make you happy?

Nan It was a long time ago.

Walker Uh-huh. . .

Nan It was just . . . so easy.

Walker (*Wistfully.*) Oh.

Nan Pip is . . . well-adjusted to the world.

Walker Oh God, well-adjusted? He's precision-manufactured; it's—

Nan *Were* you in love with him?

Walker Oh, who knows? You know, he's such a dunce, I envied him.

Nan Yes. (*Smiles.*) Yes.

Walker Nan, I took the book.

Nan I know that.

Walker I'm a completely untrustworthy person.

Nan Yes.

Walker So I was—anyway—I was reading in it?

Nan Don't tell me—

Walker It was incredible!

Nan It's always incredible—

Walker When Pip, when he said our father hated us—

Nan He said the opposite—

Walker —I couldn't get it out of my head—

Nan —besides he was talking about you, not us—

Walker I thought: Penetrating Simplicity strikes again! Then I saw this bit I hadn't seen before—

Nan Don't read it to me—

Walker I was at this wine and cheese bar—do you believe it? I found the last extant wine and—unless, it's the first *retro* wine and—anyway, they had candlelight, and this one section that I had thought was just a stain suddenly turned out to be *words*—

Nan Can't this wait till—

Walker Complete serendipity! Something about the angle of the page and the flame—like a palimpsest or pentimento or whatever you call—I had the most astonishing epiphany.

Nan Your epiphanies never mean anything—

Walker This is important—please!

Nan (*Quietly.*) . . . All right.

Walker It comes after "Theo dead." You know the punch-line of the "Theo dying" series? You have to sort of tilt the page—well, you still can't really—that's all right, I've memorized it—it says: "Theo dead. Everything I've taken from him . . ."
  Isn't that extraordinary?

Nan Huh.

Walker It's about the house, you know?

Nan I don't—

Walker No! Listen! Think about it!

Two people work together and in the end, there's no way of telling who's responsible for what. But after Theo died, nothing Ned did was any good, you see? He just coasted for thirty years. But the early stuff . . . the house . . . do you see? He didn't—you see, this is, this is *it*—he couldn't give it to us because it was never really *his*. It was all Theo's—so he left it to Pip—it's his confession, do you—"Theo dead. Everything I've taken from him." I mean it's so *so* obvious, now. That we never figured this out before!

I like to think that was kind of us.

When I realized, Nan, I started to see everything backwards through it, everything changed. It began to seem almost as if he weren't even really silent, just talking in that language I think they must use in hell, with everybody signaling wildly all the time, and no one ever picking up on any of it—do you—

Nan It's not necessarily conclusive, you know.

Walker I think it is.

Nan But it's—

Walker I *want* it to be. (*Beat.*)

Nan All right. Then it can be.

Walker Thank you. (*Beat.*)

Nan Pip wants to give you the house.

Walker He wants to—?

Nan *Sell* you, rather; he wants to sell you the house.

Walker Why?

Nan He thinks it would be good for you to have it. He *wanted* to give it to you, but I—

Walker Christ, he's unreal!

Nan I know—anyway I persuaded him to—

Walker It's like he comes from this weird other *nice* species or—

Nan I persuaded him to take money—

Walker Thank God.

Nan So. You will call him tomorrow—no: I will call him for you, and I will call Mr. Fisher, and we will set up a meeting to which you will show up promptly, and wearing a nice suit, and you will . . . have the house.

Walker I don't want it anymore.

Nan I wish I were *dead*.

Walker No.

Nan I wish I were dead—

Walker You don't—

Nan I wish . . . *you* were.

Walker That makes sense. . . . It's not the same house anymore, do you know?

Nan . . . Where will you live? Where are you . . . going to go tomorrow morning? Where—

Walker I thought here.

Nan . . . This place?

Walker For a while.

Nan *Look* at this place.

Walker Until I find something out of the city.

Nan It's no place.

Walker It's sort of random; I like that.

Nan (*Looking around.*) Oh God . . .

Walker What?

Nan I'm just trying to picture how you can possibly make this room look any worse.

Walker (*Enthusiastically.*) I *can.*
    Nan, we need to have a service!

Nan What kind of a—

Walker I missed my father's funeral—Jesus! That's shocking! We need to do something.

Nan That's all right.

Walker We *do*—what, though? It's so hard to improvise something ancient and sacred.

Nan It's impossible.

Walker No—yes—we can do it—all we need is a couple of props—

Nan Like what?

Walker Fire.

Nan Oh God, Walker, please don't burn down this building.

Walker I have the cigar! (*He finds matches.*)

Nan Don't light that—I haven't eaten—the smell—

Walker That's okay, if you throw up, it will be ceremonial. (*He goes to light the cigar, interrupts himself.*) Wait—no— first . . . (*He lays the book open on the table.*) Say good-bye . . .

Nan That's . . . corny.

Walker Come on, Nan. Say good-bye to the dead.

Nan (*A moment. Then softly.*) . . . Good-bye.

Walker Good-bye. (*A moment. Walker puts the cigar in his mouth, takes out matches, strikes a match, brings it to the cigar; wavers for a second, then suddenly, sharply, puts the match to the book.*)

Nan Jesus!

Walker Better get some water in case this thing grows—

Nan Jesus, Walker—put that out—before the whole book is gone—

Walker Too late now—

Nan Oh God—this is crazy—

Walker I feel like Hedda Gabler!

Nan Goddamn you, Walker—now we'll never know anything! (*They watch the book burn.*)

Fade out. End Act One.

Act Two

1960

The setting is the same, only enhanced, filled with color now, and the apartment has furniture.

In the apartment: Ned is quietly sketching. When he finishes a sketch, he looks at it, tears it up calmly, and throws it away; then he does it all again.

After a moment, Theo and Lina round the street corner, arguing. They stop outside the building.

Theo Don't, Lina! Do not change the subject. Do not avoid the point like this—

Lina I am avoiding nothing; there is no point, there never is with you, Theo—

Theo What incredibly noisy crap that—

Lina It *is* a choice. Either you consecrate yourself to this *vie de bohème* existence of yours or you—

Theo Jargon! Rhetoric!

Lina —or simply acknowledge that you're a young man on the make as surely as if you were working for the House of Morgan and your *architecture* is just a vehicle for your rise—

Theo (*Overlapping from "vehicle."*) What this has to do with that trashy little display you put on—at the *Plaza* for Christ's—

Lina I couldn't stand her, okay! I couldn't stand that little Farmington witch with her—Peter Pan collars and her—little string of pearls—

Theo Witch? She's a girl reporter! Ten minutes out of Mt. Holyoke or someplace! She was *inter*viewing me. She's just this nice girl—

Lina (*Morally conclusive.*) She was wearing gloves!

Theo (*Stymied a second, then.*) . . . At Condé Nast they make them—

Lina Oh, I *bet* they make them at Condé Nast.

Theo —wear *gloves*.

Lina She was gazing the entire time at your—

Theo Do you have only *one* subject?

Lina CROTCH!

Theo *Oh, Jesus!*

Lina And she hated me. She hated me.

Theo She was kind enough, Lina—generous enough to set up this interview—possibly to *place* us among the really important—

Lina Importantly well-connected—

Theo —young creative forces of our time—

Lina You're talking like the Book-of-the-Month Club, Theo. Some drivel in a magazine will not make you Christopher Wren! (*Ned, who has been listening, very still and attentive, puts his hands to his ears. Then he takes a jazz record out of its rack and puts it on the hi-fi to drown them out.*)

Theo I mean, it was *tea* at a nice hotel—why does that have to be *hard*?

Lina (*Overlapping.*) Oh and wasn't *that* an elevating locale? How interesting to discover that you can get a cup of tea at the Plaza for actually *less* than it costs to send twins through Princeton—

Theo We weren't paying, Lina; and it was going along beautifully until you decided you had to *dilate* on the wonders of the oral contraceptive. Until you decided the time was ripe for a little Joycean riff right there in the Palm Court with the *stained glass flowers.* (*Ned turns up the music some more. Theo and Lina hold their own.*)

Lina She had heard it all before, that one.

Theo Oh please—she's from this *family*—she reads expurgated Jane Austen.

Lina You know nothing. (*They're getting louder.*)

Theo God! You have me in this continuous carom between— (*Ned turns music up even more.*)

Lina You know *absolutely nothing*—

Theo . . . genital obsession and ethics.

Lina (*Between the eyes.*) You are a naive boy from the suburbs!

Theo I . . . (*This stops him. He calls into the apartment.*) Ned! (*Ned pokes his head out the window.*) I mean, would you turn down the music? Jeez, we have *neigh*bors.

Ned . . . Sorry. (*He goes back in, turns down music. Theo returns to Lina. Lina looks to him needily. He sighs, turns away a second, then goes back to her, changing the mood, cajoling.*)

Theo Hey . . . did you hear this one? (*He sings. Vaguely Lambert, Hendricks and Rossish jazz satire.*)
Joan of Arc was a woman of convictions
She never shirked a difficult situation
She thought she should save France
So she saved France
Why can't you be more like that?

(*Theo's used the song to move in on her. By the time he's through, he's holding her, kissing her neck. When the song is over, she laughs, reaches to pull his head to hers. They kiss. Ned looks up from drawing, looks out, watches, returns to drawing. When Theo and Lina start bickering again, it's more reined in at first; they're trying to sustain the mood.*)

Lina (*Coming out of the kiss.*) Why doesn't anyone know about me?

Theo Oh, *man*! What are you—

Lina Nobody knows about me—

Theo Everyone—

Lina Your parents—why—

Theo Is that what all this has been about?

Lina No! I don't know—I don't—

Theo You know the minute parents come into it, everything changes—

Lina And do we want things to stay like this?

Theo Changes for the worse. Heidegger wrote: "The light of the public always obscures."

Lina Heidegger is a famous Nazi.

Theo In the first place, you don't know. In the second place, you have to separate the work from the—

Lina Oh, what are we *talk*ing about? How wretched you are—using words like Heidegger! Are you ashamed of me?

Theo Christ, can anything happen without me being guilty of it?

Lina No, I didn't . . . you don't . . . let me—

Theo You—

Lina I mean: *Am* I something to be ashamed of?

Theo No—!

Lina No—no—don't be—easy—I *wonder* this . . . I sometimes think—

Theo (*Moving in, trying to make it intimate again.*) You think too much—

Lina I would just like something to be—

Theo You think all the time—

Lina I would like something to be . . . authentic, I can never find—

Theo It's such a beautiful night—why can't it just be—

Lina That doesn't matter—

Theo Why can't it just be a beautiful night?

Lina You have to deserve nights like this—

Theo I don't—

Lina I do—

Theo What is this? Racial guilt? The legacy of slaveowners?

Lina What a blithering idiot you are! What a fool, what a dunce! What a nightmare, what a moron! Slaveowners—we—we practically begged table scraps from sharecroppers, we—you—

Theo Lina, please—

Lina What a messed-up, delusional, romantic you are!

Theo I'm . . . I'm going to get a pizza.

Lina Theo? (*He stops.*) I sometimes don't know if I'll get through the night. (*Theo just spreads his arms: "I don't know how to answer that." He starts to walk away.*) Theo? (*He* *pauses.*) Pepperoni. (*He walks off. Lina is left alone. After a moment.*) NED! (*Ned bounds to the window.*)

Ned Y-y-yes?

Lina Are you busy? Are you in the middle of something?

Ned N-n-o.

Lina Do you want to come out and have a cigarette with me?

Ned Y-y-yes.

Lina Come out! . . . Ned?

Ned Y-y-yes?

Lina Bring cigarettes.

Ned Okay. (*He grabs cigarettes, vaults out of the apartment. When they're together.*) H-hi. (*He takes out cigarettes, hands her one.*)

Lina Light, please. (*He lights her cigarette.*) Thank you. (*She smiles. They smoke. Ned is excited to be with her, excruciatingly shy, awkward standing, awkward leaning. She smokes wonderfully.*) You must have heard us—did you hear us caterwauling before?

Ned Ye-ye-ye-no.

Lina The whole neighborhood—what fools we are, what fools. . . . I'm sorry for the disturbance. (*Ned waves it away.*) Also—because of me—it looks as though you're *not* going to be instantly translated to fame and greatness in the pages of a glossy magazine without ever having done anything to deserve it.
   I deeply apologize. (*Ned shrugs.*)
   You don't ever say much, do you?

Ned N-no.

Lina . . . You know, Moses stutter—

Ned M-Moses stuttered, I know.

He had . . . many other fine qualities, though. (*Beat. They smoke. Maybe he should go.*) . . . W-well . . .

Lina No—don't leave me. I don't want to just be standing here alone. Theo's gone to that new Italian dive to get a pizza, just stay a while.

Ned . . . All right. (*They smoke.*)

Lina We're going through a rough patch, you see.

Ned Ev-everybody—

Lina —knows?

Ned —does.

Lina Yes—that too.

It's my fault. I'm a troublemaker.

Ned No—

Lina I am. I . . . wear at him. Too emotional, too—

Ned He . . . doesn't . . . mind, he finds it . . . in-interesting.

Lina . . . Oh . . . (*Quietly.*) It isn't so interesting from inside. . . . Of course, he's no field of flowers, either. He makes as much trouble as I do, he—

Ned He's a . . . h-he's a genius.

Lina Yes . . . Naturally, I know that. I *know* he's a genius. . . . Everybody I've met in this city is a genius. And the ones that aren't are connoisseurs. How do you two manage to get along, anyway?

Ned W-w-w-w-w-w-e-e—

Lina You know, Demosthenes—

Ned Y-y-yes, I know. I know all the great . . . stu-stutterers in hi-history, I have . . . their calendar.

Lina I am sorry.

Ned No.

Lina I'm insupportable.

Ned . . . No . . .

Lina Is it true you're getting therapy for it? Theo says you're getting therapy for it.

Ned He told you that?

Lina Was he not to? Is it a secret? Are you honing your legend, too, the way Theo does? All charismatic poses and strategic suppressions?

Ned . . . I am . . . getting therapy.

Lina What does the therapy consist of?

Ned . . . Breathing.

Lina Breathing?

Ned She's teaching me to . . . b-breathe.

Lina Me, next . . .

Ned . . . as though it were my . . . b-birthright . . . she says. *Does* he h-hone his legend?

Lina Doesn't he?

Ned The . . . thing about Theo is—

Lina The thing about Theo is he's had a very poor education.

Ned Has, has he?

Lina Yes.

Ned But he's gone to—

Lina Yes, yes, I know the list of schools. It's an embarrassing list of schools. But the fact is, he's got *nothing* out of them. He's probably the best-schooled worst-educated young man on the eastern seaboard. So he's making up.

In bed, he *reads*. He reads like a man about to die who believes St. Peter gives a general information pop quiz. Last night, he read all the maxims of Rochefoucauld in forty-five minutes. You cannot do that, they're nonsense, they become . . . You start thinking you can do better yourself . . .

He's very sweet that way, but it bogs you down. Topics get too tender. Everything threatens to reveal the imposture . . .

What did you think the secret about Theo is?

Ned . . . I . . . don't recall . . . (*Pause.*)

Lina But I think without him, I'll die. (*Pause.*)

Ned He-he . . . wants things.

Lina That's true.

Ned I . . . I . . . n-never . . . m-much . . .
Theo *wants*.

Lina It's like dating Nietzsche.

Ned Wi-without him, I would . . . probably . . .

Lina I know . . .

Ned I n-never . . .
I went to . . . architecture sc-school to . . . kill time.
I . . . liked to draw.
Th-Theo took me up.
Th-this house . . . we would never have—

Lina I know.

Ned He was the b-best thing for me.
It was the b-best thing that hap-happened.

Lina I know.

Ned I . . . would die, too. (*Lina looks at him, kisses him on the cheek, rushes off.*)

Lina Theo! Theo! WHAT'S TAKING SO LONG? (*Lights.*)

(*Evening, a few days later. Ned calmly inspects a series of drawings. Theo hovers.*)

Theo It came to me *whole*. Do you know those moments? No labor, pure vision: Emerson on the I.R.T.

I started sketching right then—that's the wavery lines—anyway, you know how badly I draw, did you ever hear Cole Porter play piano? It's the same thing.

Are you looking, are you thinking, what? Don't talk. *Think*. I'm jabbering, I'll shut up. I tell you, it was such a startling thing when it came to me, I almost resisted it. I'd become comfortable with failing. I know I wasn't failing yet, but I'd started to fear . . . sterility. Delusion. Emptiness.

Don't look at that, that's corrected on the next page, see? Don't look at that, it's poorly drafted, it's a terrible idea, anyway, it stinks, I'm getting rid of it.

Listen, I'll leave you alone, I'll be silent, you'll be silent, we'll both shut up. (*Beat.*)

Why are you so quiet? Do you hate it? If you hate it, just *say* it, I'll stop already and let you . . . Of course, it's incredibly rough and, who knows, it's in progress, it's, we can throw it away. But at least we *have* something to throw away, that's the crucial step, it's when you have something you can reject completely that you know you're almost there. And it's not as if anybody else was coming up with, it's not as if you're—and of course even if it's *genius* it may not be suitable, it may not be suitable to your parents. After all it's your parents' dime we're spending (more or less literally, but) anyway, who knows what their taste is, who knows if they even *have* taste; really, there's no reason to believe they have taste at all . . .

57

Why are you looking there again? You already looked there. Is something wrong? Look, obviously all the sketches are clumsy, the arithmetic is wrong, the proportions are out of proportion, you know the minion skills I'm lousy at. Can you see the intention though?

Tell me. Tell me the truth. Tell me the absolute truth. Tell me what I want to hear. The absolute truth that I want to hear. Say nothing. *Talk.*

Ned . . . It's . . .

Theo I know it's rough.

Ned It's . . . it's not rough.

Theo But you hate it? It's ugly?

Ned No, it's . . . beautiful.

Theo You think that?

Ned I do.

Theo Ned.

Ned I've thought it for y-years.

Theo . . . What does that—?
     I don't know what that means.

Ned S-since I first saw it in a magazine.

Theo . . . In a . . . ?
     Is that *wit*?

Ned Theo, I'm sorry, but it's the Farnsworth House. (*Beat.*)

Theo What are you talking about?

Ned It's the F-Farns—

Theo No, it isn't.
     . . . It has elements in *com*mon with the Farnsworth House.

Ned Many el-elements. All of them.

Theo You don't—
   No, you don't underst—
   I will grant you—and this was on purpose—that it uses the same vo*cab*ulary—

Ned Theo, if I wrote, "To be or not . . . to be, that is the question," would you tell me it used the same vocabulary as, "To be or not to be, that . . . is the question?"

Theo Look I—
   You don't—I—
   I would even grant you that it's something of an . . . homage—

Ned Theo, it's not an homage, it's a *copy*. The funny part is, we're . . . all so van-vanguard and when we . . . copy, it's al-always the . . . most obvious p-possible thing. (*Pause.*)

Theo Not "we."

Ned What?

Theo If it's a copy, "we" didn't do it, I did.

Ned . . . Umm . . .
   I will t-take responsibility for—

Theo Or take whatever.

Ned What?

Theo No, nothing . . .

Ned Okay.
   You . . . don't have an idea, y-yet, that's . . . all right. . . .
My p-parents are p-patient and the m-money's . . . odd jobs.

Theo Mm-hmm. (*Pause. Theo picks up one of his drawings, tears it in two.*)

Ned Well, it's not as if there aren't . . . c-copies in every architecture textbook in the land. (*He picks up pieces.*) You shouldn't have d-done that, though . . . I'll t-tape it back together. God, you have a j-juvenile streak a m-mile wide.

Theo Don't bother.

Ned It's not a—

Theo What's the point? I mean, if it's—

Ned It's . . . what you said . . . The . . . thing it will be useful t-to completely . . . discard. That's progress.
   It's . . . f-fine to be . . . frustrated . . . but there's t-time.

Theo Not so much time.

Ned Time enough.
   D-don't go tearing things up. (*Pause. Theo watches Ned, who doesn't see him.*)

Theo Why do you always do this?

Ned . . . Do . . . *what*?

Theo The thing you always do.

Ned . . . Uumm . . .

Theo What you have done the last, what is it now, seven times I've attempted to—

Ned It's . . . my function.

Theo That's not it.

Ned But it is.
   That essay you're . . . forever quoting. Reynolds. Talent is divided into genius and . . . taste. We decided you would be genius and I would be . . . the other. Wh-what we must have been drinking, it's, com-completely embarrassing, but it's how things have worked out.
   If they have . . . worked out.

Theo . . . All right.

Ned What?

Theo What?

Ned *What?*
Please don't deliberately n-not . . . say some *one* thing, I—

Theo I'm not.

. . .

It's an incredible evasion, though, isn't it?

Ned What is? How?

Theo Genius and taste and Reynolds—

Ned We were drunk, but it's what—

Theo *When* was this decided?

Ned I don't—it happened.

Theo This . . . division of labor?

Ned Yes.

Theo That I would have ideas and you would destroy them?

Ned That—
Shut up. Just . . . shut up. You're making a f-fool of—

Theo That *is* what happens, though.

Ned . . . If it seems that way, then—

Theo Do you understand how *protected* that is? Do you understand how safe you are?

Ned I—

Theo Is it clear to you—do you recognize that for me everything is at risk and for you nothing?

Ned No.
No, I . . . do not understand that . . .

Listen, it's early enough—don't start.

Maybe this kind of weird, sa-sadistic rite has some kind of . . . sexual dividend . . . when it's with Lina, but I don't . . . like it—

Theo This is another evasion.

Ned If you w-want me to tell you . . . bad work is good, I . . . I won't do it . . . I'd . . . rather . . . look, why don't you just shut up, now?

Theo I don't want to—

Ned Then . . . I'm going to go for a walk.

Theo All you ever do is escape—

Ned . . . All right . . .

Theo Even the stutter is just another—

Ned (*Overlapping.*) Are you—

Theo —just another form of—

Ned You're out of your mind—

Theo Why am I the one who does the work? Why was this decided?

Ned . . . Theo—

Theo Tell me.

Ned You—

Theo Say it.

Ned . . .

You have more talent. That's . . . a given.

We've known that since . . . sc-school. We've known, ev-everybody's known that since . . .

Theo And because of that you feel compelled to punish me.

Ned We're . . . p-partners. We're . . . in business toge-to-gether. This house—my p-parents co-commissioned this house—

Theo Also hostile; also a manipulation.

Ned I'm-I'm-I'm-I'm s-sure you . . . could w-walk up and down West End Avenue and a . . . th-thousand psy-psychiatrists would agree with everything you say, but it's g-garbage and I d-don't—

Theo I just want to know why it is I'm the one who has to *pay* in this situation—

Ned Telling s-someone he's . . . more gifted than you . . . costs something—

Theo (*Overlapping.*) *Is* it just envy? And of what? Is it sex? Is it Lina? Is it me?

Ned (*Overlapping.*) I l-left home to get away from people who have no—

Theo (*Overlapping.*) I mean, was the whole point of this some kind of revenge—?

Ned (*Overlapping.*)—p-people who have no g-grace, people who are r-randomly cruel and y-you are—

Theo (*Overlapping.*) I was your friend. I am your friend. You had no other friends, I took you in—

Ned I—

Theo Who else did you have? What else did you have? Where would you be?

Ned I-I—

Theo Tell me—

Ned I-I-I—

Theo *Say* it! Just say it, Ned. *Say it*—

Ned (*He can't get his breath, he can't stop stuttering.*) I-I-I-I-I-I-I . . . (*Theo sees what's happening, is instantly remorseful, sickened.*)

Theo Oh God . . . no, don't . . . no . . . Don't try . . . it's all right . . . I'm sorry . . . I'm . . . (*Theo approaches Ned, not knowing what to do. Theo circles his arms around Ned as if to hold him, but doesn't complete the gesture.*) I'm sorry . . . Forget it . . . Please . . . forget this. . . . Please . . . please . . .

Ned It's . . . all *right*! (*Pause. They move away from each other. Beat.*)

Theo You shouldn't let me do that to you, Ned. You can't let me do that to you.

Ned I'm sorry. (*Pause.*) We d-don't . . . have to k-keep this up.

Theo We do—

Ned N-not if—

Theo What would happen to you?

Ned . . . It's not *Of Mice and Men* . . .

Theo I know that, but . . . you're better off with me.

Ned Yes.
   We say that . . . don't we? (*Pause.*)

Theo I'm going to go away for a while. I need to . . .
   I'll go to my parents' shack in—

Ned Okay.

Theo Someplace I can work. (*Beat.*) You're right. . . . That was shit. That was . . . shit. (*Beat.*) Meanwhile, none of this ever happened. Okay?

Ned Yes. . . . Fine. (*They look at each other, smile tentatively. Theo turns away. Ned stares at his back. Fade out.*)

(In black: the sound of a heavy rain. The rain continues. The light in the apartment is that cocoonish light that comes sometimes on rainy afternoons, a muted array of the colors at the end of the spectrum. There's a fuss at the door. Ned offstage.)

Ned I'll—

Lina Ooh—I'm shaking it's—

Ned H-here's the key—

Lina Wonderful! *(Key in the lock; they enter, Ned has a grocery bag.)* I'm going to drip all over your nice, dilapidated floor!

Ned Th-that's—me, too.

Lina That was gorgeous, wasn't it?

Ned Yes. . . . G-give me your slicker. *(Lina takes her slicker off and hands it to Ned.)* You're soaked through.

Lina I don't mind. Oh, there aren't any blazing fires here, are there? I forget—

Ned No.

Lina Just banked ones *(This is a playful reference to Ned: he doesn't quite catch it.)*—no, nothing.

Ned Y-you're going to catch cold or—

Lina No, I don't. Isn't that moment thrilling, right before it starts, and everything turns purple and the awnings shake and the buildings ignite from the inside? I love that part.

Ned If you . . . n-need to change—

Lina I don't mind just sopping for a while. But is there bourbon?

Ned I . . . No, I don't—

Lina There must be.

Ned S-sorry, I—

Lina I happen to know there is.

Ned . . . There is? (*Lina goes to a box on top of a stack of books next to the drafting table and extracts a bottle.*)

Lina Theo is not a big *sharer*.

Ned N-no.

Lina Do you want some? (*Ned waves a hand, "I pass."*) You ought to. It makes everything *so* much better.

Ned Everything's . . . fine.

Lina Is it?

Ned . . . Today, yes. (*She sips the drink she's poured.*)

Lina Yes. For me, too.
    It was funny running into you.

Ned Yes!

Lina I didn't even realize I was here! I didn't even realize I'd come to this neighborhood. It was not my intention.

Ned What was?

Lina I didn't have one.

Ned M-me, neither.

Lina I was off from the bookstore. I just wandered away the day.

Ned Th-Theo left his robe.

Lina . . . Uuuhhh . . . well. Segue?

Ned I'm worried about you . . . in those things.

Lina You are just desperate to get me out of my clothes, aren't you?

Ned I . . . don't want you to get sick.

Lina . . . Where's the robe?

Ned In the bathroom. On the hook.

Lina I'll change. (*Crosses to bathroom.*) You can change in here when I do. I promise I won't look.

Ned I'm fine.

Lina I promise I won't.

Ned I'm not as wet as you.

Lina No, that's right, I'm *all* wet. Let me bring my drink. (*Passing him.*) I've seen this scene before, you know. (*She goes into the bathroom, keeping the door open a crack. Ned starts unpacking bags onto counter, an array of vegetables, picked for color. Lina calls from bathroom.*) Hey!

Ned What?

Lina Say something small to me while I'm changing!

Ned W-what?

Lina Just chatter at me! I get restless!

Ned I . . . d-don't know what to say.

Lina Just nonsense . . . palaver.

Ned Oh. (*Pause.*) D-do you believe in Original Sin? (*Half-beat. She pokes her head around the door.*)

Lina (*As though answering his question.*) No, in fact, I don't believe I *have* seen any good movies lately. Why—have *you*?

Ned Oh . . . no. (*Lina emerges in robe.*)

Lina Original Sin!

Ned I—

Lina It's like tea chat with Reinhold Niebuhr.
Why. Do you?

Ned Um, yes, let's change the subject—

Lina No, it's interesting to me—

Ned It's not.

Lina It's just I've grown unaccustomed to the idea—

Ned It's peculiar.

Lina With Theo, there are never any ghosts of any kind.
Never any clouds or impediments. He's all sort of sharp and
slender and gleaming . . .

Ned . . . He's . . .

Lina . . . Rather a me*tal*lic young man . . .

Ned He's . . . (*Pause.*)

Lina (*Mostly to herself.*) But I swore I wouldn't do that today
. . . (*Brightening deliberately.*) What a beautiful harvest on
that countertop!

Ned I . . . liked the colors.

Lina Are you going to just leave them there to look at?
They'll rot.

Ned No, I—

Lina Or make dinner? I'm not *ang*ling.

Ned . . . I thought I'd m-make dinner. (*Awkward moment.*)

Lina I'll leave when the rain lets up a little.

Ned N-no.

Lina Yes, I will.

Ned Your clothes have to dry.

Lina I can wear them damp.

Ned . . . All right. (*He gets a knife, starts chopping vege-tables. With sudden gallantry.*) Won't you please stay to dinner?

Lina Give me that knife. (*He yields it. She starts chopping what he was chopping. After a moment, she starts sniffing the air.*) I've always rather *enjoyed* the smell of drenched wool on a person. (*He whips off his sweater. Lights.*)

(*Rain louder. Half-hour later. They're finishing dinner.*)

Lina That was spectacular!

Ned It was . . . just a salad.

Lina No. It was like some fall-of-Rome variation on a salad. Every leaf, every herb, every pepper stick, it was Trimalchian.

Ned Th-thank you.

Lina No, thank *you*. . . . What time is it, do you know?

Ned The c-clock is broken. Early, though. M-maybe seven? If the rain lets up, we can . . . s-see a movie later, if you like.

Lina Yes, we could go out. What's playing?

Ned Mm . . . D-down the block, there's *The World of Suzie Wong*.

Lina Or we could stay in.

Ned Either way. Here. (*He pours her the last of the wine, hands it to her, smiles. He's about to say something.*)

Lina What?

Ned Nothing . . . I'm . . . so happy; it's weird.

Lina (*Puzzled by it.*) Yes! I know, me too!

Ned All day—

Lina Yes, me too! . . . I usually wake in what they call a "brown study." I have no idea what that means but I love to say it—"brown study"—but today . . . I got up and it wasn't raining yet but there was already the scent of it, and I had nothing at all to do. I made some coffee and lit a cigarette and read the dire newspaper and thought, well, all right, yes, give me another sixty years of this.

Ned I—yes—

Lina The two of us waking in a mood like that on the same morning—it's a statistical exorbitance! Given our natures.

Ned Yes—

Lina We have to figure it out: What different thing did our days have in common? (*Pause. They look at each other; a sad recognition neither wants to say aloud.*)

Ned I'll clear the plates. (*He starts to.*)

Lina Let me help you—

Ned No . . . I can.

Lina . . . Okay. (*She sits, lights a cigarette, while Ned cleans off the dishes.*) Has he called you today?

Ned Y-yes.

Lina Oh . . . and how is everything?

Ned He-he's . . . working v-very hard. Apparently, he's had, um, a brainstorm and—

Lina Oh . . . good . . .

Ned Yes . . . he . . . s-says, he's f-finally onto . . . the real thing . . . he n-needed to get away and it's . . . c-come at last. . . . When he comes b-back, we'll have to . . . p-play the March from "Scipio" or s-something . . .
    Hasn't he called you?

Lina Yes. Well, I think so. I'm not sure.

Ned What?

Lina Well, this morning, when I was reading the paper, the phone rang and rang for . . . ten minutes, I think. That was probably him.

Ned Oh. . . . Would you like coffee?

Lina I would dearly love some coffee. (*Ned starts to prepare some.*) Anyway, what did you do today?

Ned It was . . . nothing . . . the same as y-you.

Lina Tell me anyway.

Ned I don't—

Lina I'm getting that feeling—just talk, talk . . . talk it away.

Ned . . . What? Um . . . okay . . . (*They look at each other.*) It was . . . same as you.

I slept . . . late this morning and when I woke up, it was . . . already raining a little.

And I felt so . . . light. Free, the way I n-never do. I went to the c-corner to buy coffee and a roll . . . and the pavement was slick and . . . jet in places and the sidewalk was this oily brown in places and . . . there were two women in identical trench coats. One of them h-had just bought an African violet plant and she kept tilting it so dirt kept falling on her . . . feet and . . . it s-surprised her each time so each t-time she would apologize to her . . . shoes, which I liked. I bought the coffee and sipped it and I . . . d-didn't come home right away. I walked out of my way because it was all so . . . pleasant, the day.

I felt like a . . . flaneur.

Lina What's a flaneur?

Ned Don't you know that word?

71

Lina No. I don't know that word.

Ned A flaneur is a wanderer through the city. Someone who . . . idles through the streets without a purpose . . . except to idle through the streets. And linger when it, when it . . . pleases him.

Lina That's what he does?

Ned Yes.

Lina What about work? Does he ever get to work?

Ned He has no work . . . if he's the real thing.

Lina He just strolls?

Ned Yes. It's his career.
 He has a . . . private income.

Lina Some vast sum.

Ned P-pennies but they . . . suffice. He d-doesn't need . . . much. Not what people need who have . . . intricate lives. He just .. walks, you see. His life has no pattern . . . just traffic . . . and no hope—

Lina That's sad—

Ned Because he has no n-need of hope! The only thing he wants from life is . . . the day at hand. And when he's old . . . his memories aren't of Triumphs and Tragedies. He remembers . . . certain defunct cafes where he shared cups of coffee with . . . odd, scary strangers. And people he's known for years and years. Slightly.

Lina Because it's a solitary thing to be a *flaneur*.

Ned Yes . . . but never lonely . . . I think.

Lina Is that what you want to be?

Ned I haven't g-got the strength of character. But it's what I would w-wish . . . for someone better than I am. I think it would be the best thing! To be this . . . vagabond prince. Do you know? A wanderer through the city.

A walker. (*Beat.*)

Lina Tell me about this house you two are making.

Ned No.

Lina Theo never does.

Ned It's . . . idiotic—

Lina It isn't, it's exciting, it makes me want to—

Ned . . . What?

Lina —want to *be* something. I want to be . . . a painter!

Ned You do?

Lina Or . . . a writer, a *belletrist*!

Ned Oh.

Lina Or a Negro blues singer or just a very intriguing alcoholic. . . . I am so terribly old.

Ned You're young!

Lina I'm a Southern woman who admits to thirty—God alone knows what the truth of things must be!

Ned You're an in-infant.

Lina I'm *nothing*.

Ned You're lovely—

Lina (*On "lovely."*) Theo looks at me and sees . . . something from Anaïs Nin. Just because I'm gloomy, sometimes, and opaque, sometimes. And because when he picked me up, we were sketching naked men at the Art Students League. These sorts of things impress him. He is so naive; he is so easily astonished. He sees me as one of those girls from fifteen years ago: all Quattrocento-pale and dull-eyed and glazed and smugly silent because they possess the secret of the universe and you don't. *I* don't. That's what's funny—I am *never* silent—he must notice that. I smother the day in speech because I know nothing and I want someone to speak back to me and *tell* me—what?

What is it that some people in cities seem to know? What is this secret that is constantly eluding me?

Ned (*Suddenly.*) There isn't any.

Lina ... What?

Ned There isn't any s-secret. I used to ... think that, too ... but, no ... no secret to be found ... just ... g-gestures ... whims ... energy ... personality, do you know?

Lina (*Mordant, but serious.*) That's tragic.

Ned Is it? I thought ... it was nice ... when I realized. A relief.

Lina And when was that?

Ned So recently.

Lina Still ... I want something. ... I suppose I'll marry Theo and that will be something—

Ned (*Abrupt.*) Is that happening?

Lina Nobody ever says anything, but ... what else?

I'm so happy for you, that you have this house, that you're beginning something—

Ned I'm not ... happy about—

Lina But—

Ned It's going to ... explode in our faces.

Lina No.

Ned We're . . . we *are* too young, m-much too young, no one has . . . ever d-done this so young. We should still be . . . hirelings . . . doing . . . rest rooms and el-elevator shafts, but Theo—

Lina Theo—

Ned He . . . *wants*. No one will ever commission us.

Lina But this *house*—

Ned My p-parents. My parents. No indication at all.

Lina But then you'll have this house and people will see it and come to you.

Ned *I-if* we have it; we're . . . waiting on Theo who's . . . waiting on God who's . . . blocked.

  Theo's been a little st-stalled since school and until he gets an idea that's real—

Lina But you said he claims to have one.

Ned . . . Y-yes. He does.

Lina That makes you sad.

Ned No.

Lina It does, though. Why does *he* have to have the idea?

Ned (*Slightly strict.*) Because that's how it is.

  Who knows what will come of this anyway? If I minded the prospect of catastrophic failure, I never would have started the whole thing. . . . This is what I imagine will happen: . . . My parents . . . will invest most of the money they have in this h-house . . . as a way of m-making up . . . and the house will never be built . . . or if it is b-built . . . it will collapse due to some mysterious and in-incalculable . . . design flaw. And we will all end up . . . dead. And bankrupt . . . strewn along . . . v-various gutters.

  I see this with . . . astonishing clarity.

Bru-brutal clarity. Poverty. Hunger. Aban-bandonment. Incorporated. (*Beat*.) In my . . . darkest midnight hours, I . . . have this theory that . . . (*With one hand, he describes a column*.) Here are . . . our intentions . . . and here . . . (*With the other hand, a parallel column*.) is what actually happens . . . and the only thing spanning them (*He connects the two columns on top with an arc*.) is Guilt.

Lina Guilt?

Ned The . . . preposterous instinct that we are . . . wholly re-responsible for events . . . completely out of our control. (*He makes the shapes again*.)
     What we want . . . what we get . . . guilt: It's an arch.

Lina What you want . . . (*She does a line at a fairly low level*.) What you will get . . . (*She makes a parallel line at her full reach*.) Genius . . . (*A soaring line connecting the two*.) It's a . . . Flight Path. An Ascent!

Ned (*Blushes, smiles*.) That's sentimental. . . .
     Thank you. (*Beat*.)

Lina You are such a nice man.
     This has been such a wonderful day!
     We have to . . . I want to . . . If only we really knew *how* to . . .

Ned What?

Lina Cherish . . . this easy moment . . . when we mean so little to each other. (*Pause*.)

Ned I think the coffee's ready.

Lina . . . Oh . . . oh, yes! (*Ned crosses to the kitchenette*.) I think . . . the rain. . . . The rain seems to have let up a little. Maybe I should . . . skip the coffee and take advantage of—

Ned Your clothes, though . . . They may not be . . .

Lina Yes, but they may be—

Ned I'll check for you. (*He goes into bathroom, emerges a moment later. A little sadly.*) Oh. They are.

Lina Oh

. . .

I suppose I really ought to . . .

Ned All right. (*They smile, awkwardly; she crosses to the bathroom, takes her clothes off the curtain rod, and, leaving the door slightly open, starts to change.*) Lina.

Lina (*Pokes head out.*) Yes?

Ned Oh. I just wanted to see . . . if I could . . . say your name . . . without fumbling it.
And I did: L-L-L . . . Lina.

Lina Yes. You did. (*Hesitation. She goes back into bathroom. Ned just stands there. Lina can be glimpsed, shaking dry her clothes. Ned starts to say something. Changes his mind. A moment. He speaks.*)

Ned I'm always w-watching you.
Whenever you're here . . . I can't help it. I try not to. Ev-ever since I met you.
It's awful. . . . I don't want it. . . . I d-don't expect . . . to have things . . . like other people, but I'm . . . always th-thinking of you. It's h-horrible . . .
I kn-know nothing can come of it . . . I know I can't have . . . the things I w-want. I shouldn't tell you this. I ca-can't stop, though. I'm sorry. I'm so sorry.
You're s-so . . . fantastic, you're . . . D-don't let him t-take you down . . . the way he does. Don't let him . . . hurt you. You don't de-deserve it. You deserve only good things. N-not him. Not me. Or . . . I mean, not—(*By now, she has returned to the room. She looks at him.*)

Lina You're just . . . talking on and on—

Ned No.

Lina You are.

Ned I don't waste words. I can't . . . afford to. (*A moment.*) I didn't say anything—

Lina But you did—

Ned F-forget it—

Lina I don't want to. (*The rain is louder now.*) Look—it's started again!
　A downpour. (*Lights.*)

(*Two days later. The rain continues. Morning. First light. Theo appears in a neutral space—somewhere in the city— thrashing through the rain. He stops as though paralyzed, then moves on. Once he's exited, lights come up in the apartment, revealing Ned and Lina in bed.*)

Lina Was there a moment when you knew how you wanted to spend the rest of your life? Was there a day?

Ned Um, yes, actually. Why?

Lina Tell me.

Ned I was about . . . fifteen. And I wanted to spend the day in the park—Central—the park. I brought a sketch pad because I was afraid somebody might want to talk to me. And—I drew the buildings I was looking up at. Then for no reason I started m-making up my own. And the day was so beautiful, I thought I must be talented. So I kept it up.

Lina What do *I* want?
　You right now in this bed forever.
　I want that.
　And children.

Ned Children?

Lina Well . . . one child, at least. One beautiful little girl. Someone precious I can drink with.

Ned I don't like them, much. Ch-children.

Lina . . . No one nice ever says that.

Ned I-I don't feel so bad about it. Plenty of other people l-like them. And most children grow up, so it's not as though I've decided against anyone f-for all time.

Lina How can you not like them, though?

Ned I just . . . n-never know what to say to them. I . . . never was a child . . . much my . . . self and they sc-scare me.

Lina Because they always tell the truth? People say children always tell—

Ned No . . . I don't think they tell the truth. P-people say they tell the truth but . . . those people are stupid. I don't think children are truthful, just . . . terribly candid. Whenever I'm with one I'm afraid it's g-going to point at me and say something humiliating.
   Plus, they're boring.
   Intensely boring.
   And you're constantly being forced to marvel at the tedious things they do. "Johnny counted to five today! F-five!" I don't know what to say to that. I stand there. P-people hate me for that. By the time Johnny gets to t-ten, I'm out of their lives.
   But if you want a child, we can have one. (*Beat.*) But you were talking . . . in the abstract, weren't you?

Lina Theories the-theoretically are turning into facts very quickly these days. (*They look at each other. Ned wanders over to the drafting table. Lina gets up, puts on robe, tidies the bed a bit or just idles in it. Ned rips a sketch in two. She goes to him, takes the pieces of the sketch from him.*) What are you doing? What is that?

Ned It's nothing—just something I did.

Lina But it's beautiful.

Ned I like to . . . tear them up.

Lina It's remarkable!

Ned Just . . . something I did . . .

Lina How amazing you are. (*While she studies the ripped sketch, Ned takes out a fresh notebook, writes something in it, then closes the book.*) What is *that*?

Ned Nothing.

Lina What *is* that?

Ned (*Shakes his head.*) Nothing.

Lina (*Playful.*) *Tell* me!

Ned It's a journal.

Lina A diary?

Ned No. A journal?

Lina What's the difference?

Ned I'm a boy.

Lina You keep a journal?

Ned Only when I'm happy.

Lina (*Holds out hand.*) Let me.

Ned But—

Lina *Let* me. (*Ned hands it over.*) It's brand-new.

Ned First time I'm happy.

Lina (*Reads.*) "April 3rd to April 5th: Three days of rain." (*She looks up at him.*) That's all?

Ned Sufficient.

Lina But—

Ned I'll know what it means. (*He pulls her toward him.*)

Lina Let me go! I'm going to make breakfast! I'm going to *cook*!

Ned You have that skill?

Lina I've been known to soft-boil an egg in my day. That is, if you have any eggs.

Ned I think there's a couple left over from . . . Christmas or s-something.

Lina Then I'll *hard*-boil them. (*Key in the door. Theo enters.*) Theo. (*Theo looks at her.*)

Ned Theo.
   Hi. You weren't supposed to get back till—
   Lina's here.
   We ran into each other, we s-saw a movie—the rain—she stayed.
   You said you were c-coming back tonight. (*Pause.*)

Theo I'm just dropping off my stuff. (*Theo puts down the bag he's carrying, then walks out. Hesitation. Ned starts out after him.*)

Lina Ned? (*Outside.*)

Ned Theo—

Theo I don't want to talk, Ned.

Ned Theo, listen—

Theo I can't talk yet—

Ned But we—

Theo Just leave me alone—

Ned Look—

Theo I can't—see you—

Ned Theo please . . .

Theo *I didn't bring anything back, okay?* (*Beat.*)

Ned . . . Wh-what?

Theo I don't have anything.
  I didn't do the job.

Ned Oh . . . (*A moment. Almost laughing.*) Oh!

Theo I *can't* do this job, Ned. (*Beat.*)

Ned Of course you can.

Theo Don't tell me that anymore!
  Don't tell me I can, then explain why I haven't.
  Don't—
  I keep—
  You were right—I've let everybody down—I've hurt every-
body.

Ned I never said—

Theo I think I made the wrong choice.
  I'm sorry.

Ned Don't apolo— *God*—don't—look—come inside. We'll
 . . . have breakfast or something—we'll talk—

Theo I can't go in there.

Ned Well what are you going to do?

Theo I don't know.
  I'll go someplace.
  Washington Square Park or—

Ned In *this*?

Theo . . . someplace. Oh, look, I'll be fine, okay? Just don't tell Lina about any of this. Promise you won't—

Ned But—

Theo Oh, shit. I'm not here, okay? None of this happened, we didn't talk—

Ned Theo—

Theo (*Desperate.*) How was the movie?

Ned . . . What?

Theo Please?

Ned . . .
S-so-so. (*A moment.*)

Theo Good. (*Ned looks at Theo. Ned turns back to go into the apartment, then turns back to Theo.*)

Ned Theo?

Theo No—
This will be fine.
Truly. (*Ned returns inside. Theo puts his head up to the rain, soaks in it. Then he stands for a while, uncertain where to go. A moment.*)

Ned Oh, Jesus.

Lina Did you tell him?

Ned (*Amazed; working through the scene that's just happened.*) It didn't . . . come up.

Lina Oh!

Ned That wasn't . . . the t-topic.

Lina How funny.
No.
He seemed too intense to be thinking about me.

Ned He didn't bring anything back.

Lina I didn't imagine he had.

Ned He said he can't . . . do this job.

Lina Well.
  There will be other jobs.

Ned God! He's just . . . walking around—

Lina That's all right.

Ned But—

Lina That can be useful.

Ned Oh, man—what I've done!

Lina You have done nothing—

Ned What I've done to him . . . it's like a s-sin—

Lina These puritan categories—they *dom*inate you—

Ned I—

Lina It's fine . . . it's for the best.

Ned What will he d-do?

Lina He's a handsome young man in Manhattan, *something* will happen to him.

Ned B-but—

Lina Oh, this is *Theo*—he will be sad for a minute and then *not* sad. Nothing stops Theo. (*Theo disappears around the corner.*)

Ned I've ruined your life. (*Lina holds him, buries her head in his neck.*)

Lina You've-saved-me-you've-saved-me-you've-saved-me.

Ned (*Softly.*) Oh, I hope so.

Lina I *know*. (*The rain lightens. Lina looks right at Ned.*) Begin.

Ned What?

Lina The house. Begin the house. (*Beat. Ned lets out a nervous laugh.*)

Ned No.

Lina I know you see it. I know you see the whole thing. Don't you?

Ned Yes.
   I know every moment.

Lina Then what are you waiting for?

Ned I don't want to—

Lina *Some*body has to.

Ned I'll . . . *hire* somebody . . .

Lina Neddie—

Ned Things . . . are so much better . . . before they actually start.

Lina Edmund.

Ned Oh. . . . Let's . . . have breakfast . . . d-didn't you say you were going to fix us some—let's go back to bed—

Lina Later. That will be your reward. I'll be your muse!

Ned Oh, Lina.

Lina Oh, *look*—an hour from now I'll cook us a simply wretched breakfast, and we'll sit together and plan what to tell Theo when he gets back, and wallow in remorse, and plot every second of the next two hundred years but *this minute*: turn around. Just draw something. Make a home. (*He turns* *around, picks up a pencil, finds a fresh sheet of paper. He makes a first mark.)*

Ned The beginning . . . of error. (*Lina smiles. Ned continues. Lights fade out.*)

END OF PLAY.

The American Plan

THE AMERICAN PLAN is for Helen Merrill
and Evan Yionoulis.

The American Plan was first produced by Manhattan Theatre Club Stage II (Lynne Meadow, Artistic Director; Barry Grove, Managing Director) on January 23, 1990, in New York City. It was directed by Evan Yionoulis; the scene design was by James Youmans; the costume design was by Jess Goldstein; the lighting design was by Donald Holder; original music and sound was by Thomas Cabaniss; and the production stage manager was Richard Hester. The cast was as follows:

Lili Adler Rebecca Miller
Nick Lockridge Tate Donovan
Olivia Shaw Beatrice Winde
Eva Adler Joan Copeland
Gil Harbison Eric Stoltz

The American Plan was moved to the mainstage of the Manhattan Theatre Club on December 4, 1990. The cast was as follows:

Lili Adler Wendy Makkena
Nick Lockridge D. W. Moffett
Olivia Shaw Yvette Hawkins
Eva Adler Joan Copeland
Gil Harbison Jonathan Walker

Act One

SCENE ONE. *Lili lies in hammock, reading a book. Nick enters in bathing trunks, from a swim. He lifts a towel from the grass, starts drying himself off, discovers Lili.*

Nick Oh . . . hi!

Lili Hi.

Nick I just took a swim.

Lili I can see.

Nick What a pleasure!—I didn't notice you here before.

Lili I just came out to read a book.

Nick I won't disturb you, then.

Lili Please do. It's a horribly tedious book.

Nick My name's Nicky Lockridge.

Lili Lili Adler.

Nick Pleased to meet you.

Lili Yes . . . I'd been hoping to.

Nick What?

Lili I've seen you. . . . I've seen you around.

Nick Oh.

Lili Is that the wrong sort of thing to say?

Nick Not at all.

Lili I sometimes say the wrong sorts of things—

Nick Not this time.

Lili Thank you.

Nick Have you been here long?

Lili Forever. Mostly, I stay on this side of the lake.

Nick I can understand the temptation.

Lili . . . What do you mean?

Nick Things get a little, well, a little hectic, huh, on the other side?

Lili As I said, I seldom go.

Nick Of course you did. Wonderful swimming in this lake, though. I don't know why people don't use it. Everybody's always hopping into the pool at the hotel, but this lake—it's gorgeous!

Lili It's infested.

Nick What?

Lili With snakes, water moccasins.

Nick Funnily enough, I missed them.

Lili No, of course I'm making it up. So what brings you to the Catskills?

Nick It's my vacation. I'm here with some friends.

Lili Why?

Nick . . . It's someplace different.

Lili Yes, it is. And what do you do?

Nick —Um—

Lili For work.

Nick Oh, I . . . I'm planning to be an architect.

Lili Well, everyone has pipe-dreams. What do you do at present?

Nick I more-or-less write. (*Beat.*) I'm more-or-less a magazine writer . . . at present.

Lili Do you more-or-less write for any more-or-less specific periodical?

Nick Yes . . . I write for the *Weekly Cultural Epiphany*.

Lili Never heard of it.

Nick Mostly, we spot trends and lionise masterpieces, that sort of—

Lili The *Weekly Cultural Epiphany*—I've never—

Nick I write for *Time*.

Lili Oh. (*With recognition.*) Oh! (*Beat.*) *You* know, I've never in my life known anyone actually to *read Time*—

Nick Well—

Lili But everyone I meet these days seems to write for it.

Nick That's—

Lili I've begun to believe that *Time* magazine doesn't exist. It's in fact this vast conspiracy designed to lend credibility to the unemployed—

Nick That may well—

Lili I see these men on the street—drunk—sleeping— befouled—I think, "Oh, look they work for *Time!*"—

Nick Well—

Lili No, really, I'm sure it's a very worthwhile job.

Nick I can assure you it isn't. And what do you do?

Lili I—well—I. (*Beat.*) I'm pre-occupational.

Nick Are you a student?

Lili . . . I have been.

Nick Where?

Lili I attended Sarah Lawrence College.

Nick Oh. (*With comprehension.*) Oh!

Lili You're thinking, "That's why she's crazy."

Nick Not at all.

Lili Anyway, I didn't stay long.

Nick Why was that?

Lili (*Quietly.*) Another day, another day. . . . Anyway, feel free to make yourself at home here.

Nick (*Puzzled.*) I do.

Lili It's relaxing, don't you find?

Nick Oh, yes. Especially, after, you know . . . over there.

Lili Are you getting tired of things?

Nick Well, the American Plan—*what* Americans live like this? What Americans *eat* like this? The breakfasts and the lunches and the dinners and the coffees and the teas and the snacks and the hardly-any-exercise in-between . . .

Lili And are you getting tired at all of Mindy? (*Beat.*)

Nick I beg your . . . umm . . . Excuse me?

Lili You're with Mindy Kahkstein, aren't you?

Nick Well . . .

Lili I've seen you together . . .

Nick We—

Lili She hangs onto you like you're, I don't know, a Blue Chip stock or something—

Nick We're together.

Lili Huh!

Nick ... How did you know?

Lili I go over there sometimes.

Nick Ah!

Lili We're not actually with the hotel, but my mother thinks it's good for me to ... mingle, to observe.

Nick You're here with your mother?

Lili Forever. You can see her if you squint.

Nick Where?

Lili Across the lake. Right next to—oh look, quel surprise! It's Mindy!

Nick Where's Mindy?

Lili A little to the left of where you're looking, now. See? The one with the turbulent thighs and the exotic swimsuit—she kind of looks like she came dressed in a Rhonda Fleming movie?

Nick Oh, yes!

Lili Well, my mother is the one to her right. That looming, late-Ibsenesque figure with the Mah Jong tiles. Oh, and right next to my mother—the Negro woman? That's Olivia—she's ours.

Nick What does Olivia do?

Lili She endures.

Nick What?

Lili She cleans.

Nick Oh.

Lili Cooks a little, listens to my mother's tirades. "One of the well-spoken colored," my mother calls her. This is a step up from "schvartzes."

Nick Your mother's the one they call, "the Duchess," isn't she?

Lili I wouldn't be the least surprised, the way she treats them. People like my mother never come to the Catskills. She's only here because she thinks you should always have a population you can feel superior to—she's really a dreadful woman.

Nick I'm sure not.

Lili Why—what do you know?

Nick Well, if she were so dreadful, it's unlikely she'd have reared such a . . . charming . . . and mercurial daughter. (*Beat.*)

Lili Protestant!

Nick Guilty as charged. (*Looks across lake.*) Oh my God, they're playing more Simon Says. What a nightmare.

Lili Simon Says: A witless unseen despot who derives his authority from God-knows-where instructs you to deform yourself in truly revolting ways; and if you dare, even accidentally, to act without his permission, you're exterminated. My mother thinks it's a great game for Jews.

Nick I'm sorry—but I don't find that funny.

Lili But my mother *is* a Jew—

Nick All the same. (*Beat.*)

Lili (*Vulnerably.*) I'm sorry.

Nick You don't have to apologize—

Lili I do—

Nick There's nothing to apologize *for*—

Lili Please don't lose respect for me so soon—(*Beat. He looks at her—kindly and puzzled.*) *So*—Mindy's an education major, isn't she?

Nick Yes, I think so.

Lili Yes. Those girls are. How did you come to know her?

Nick She goes to N.Y.U. We met at Washington Square Park. Or the Automat. A museum, I forget. New York is one big mixer.

Lili Her father, I believe, pioneered broadloom in Central New Jersey.

Nick Something like that.

Lili But do you find her *droll*?

Nick She's—

Lili Because I've known Mindy for many summers, and, in my experience, I don't believe I've ever heard anyone describe her as *droll*.

Nick In my experience, I don't believe I've ever heard anyone describe *anyone* as droll.

Lili . . . Touché . . .

Nick She's a very nice girl. I like her a lot.

Lili She's extremely rich. (*Beat.*)

Nick And who says I'm not? (*Beat.*)

Lili Then why do you work?

Nick What do you mean?

Lili You hate your job. Why don't you quit?

Nick Because you have to work.

Lili Not if you have money, you don't.

Nick Yes, you do.

Lili Why?

Nick Because.

Lili Why?

Nick It's not a thing to question. Why do you even question it? (*Beat.*) Why are you looking at me like that?

Lili I like the way you look.

Nick I'm flattered.

Lili Like nothing ever happened to you.

Nick I don't know if that's such a good thing . . .

Lili It's a very good thing, believe me, a *very* good thing. So, is it true that Mindy's a nymphomaniac?

Nick (*Pauses, bemused, shocked, amazed at her effrontery, then:*) Yes.

Lili *Really?*. . . A *big* one?

Nick They only come in one size.

Lili Is that. . . . Well, is that *fun*?

Nick It depends—

Lili On what—?

Nick The time of day, the—oh, look, this isn't something I'm really comfortable talking about—

Lili (*Quickly.*) I'm sorry—

Nick Maybe I should just go back—

Lili No—no—absolutely not—

Nick No, it's been very pleasant talking with you—

Lili (*A desperate staying tactic.*) Where do you live? (*Beat.*)

Nick Where do I live?

Lili Your New York residence? In New York?

Nick In the Village. For *now*. This little place in the Village. Where do you live?

Lili The river Styx. (*Beat.*) This place on Central Park West. Where the rooms are heavy with dark damask and filled with a sabbath light—

Nick Uh-huh—

Lili Which is not light at all, but merely darkness visible—

Nick You live in New York's only Miltonic co-op—

Lili . . . You recognized.

Nick I went to good schools.

Lili Anyway, it's a horrible place, and sort of disgraces us. It's the doctors and the intellectuals who got to live on Park Avenue. My father's profession didn't rate.

Nick Oh, what did he do?

Lili Before my mother murdered him, he was an inventor of some kind.

Nick That's not true—

Lili Oh, yes, he invented—well, I've never actually been sure, but it is very lucrative—

Nick Your mother did not murder your father.

Lili Oh, yes. With small doses of cyanide administered in his farina. Cyanide was flavorless so—

Nick Cyanide tastes like almonds—

Lili Oh; you've dabbled?

Nick It's a well-known. . . . Dabbled! . . . It's a well-known . . . I read mysteries.

Lili She killed him, but bribed the law up-and-down . . . she has the scratch for it . . . and now she's holding me captive here.

Nick Yes. And why is that?

Lili She's terribly disappointed in me. . . . She'd always hoped for an attractive daughter. She thinks I was some sort of genetic mutation.

Nick That can't be it—

Lili But it is!

Nick No one could ever feel shortchanged by *your* looks. (*Beat.*)

Lili (*Softly.*) Thank you. (*Beat.*) Or yours. You look like—

Nick Nothing ever happened to me, I know—

Lili It's your charm! Nicky Tabula-Rasa, that's what I'll call you!

Nick Please don't.

Lili It's a good name!

Nick It's the wrong name . . .

Lili I don't think so.

Nick Trust me.

Lili (*Softly.*) I don't think so. (*Pause. They look at each other. Offstage: Eva's voice calls musically: "Lili . . . Lili! . . ."*) Oh God!

Nick Who is that?

Lili Her. She's come back.

Nick So?

Lili She's going to send Olivia for me now. Or come herself. She'll take me back to the house.

Nick The house?

Lili Yes. Over there.

Nick Is that—is that yours?

Lili Yes. Of course.

Nick Where we are now—is this your property?

Lili Yes. (*Beat. Nick colors, starts foraging for his clothes.*)

Nick God, I'm sorry—I'm very sorry—I had no idea.

Lili No—no—it's fine—

Nick If I had known, I'd never have . . . just sprawled out here like this—

Lili Don't go—

Nick It's just . . . that house doesn't even look like a house, really, I thought it was . . . I don't know . . . a boathouse or something . . . and it certainly doesn't seem to go along with this land and so I—I'm very, *very* sorry—

Lili Stop. Please . . . stop. (*He is dressed by now; he stops, looks at her.*) Look—Please—would you please—come see me sometimes? There's no one—I don't speak to anyone—and they're—they're very stern with me and—oh, please, would you, would you please . . . come see me?

Nick Lili—

Lili Just while you're here. Just sometimes. (*Olivia enters, stands a little away from them.*)

Olivia (*Gently.*) Lili . . . (*Lili looks at her, looks back at Nick Then she goes to Nick, takes his face in her hands, and kisses him. They part and she walks off with Olivia. Nick stands there.*)

Fade Out. End of Scene.

SCENE TWO. *Lili, Eva, and Olivia are breakfasting outside.*

Eva . . . And, then, we all repaired to the club where the most mystifying entertainer held forth . . . if only I could remember his name! . . . He was . . . how do you say it . . . *crossed-eyed,* with vast jowls and this idiotic, juvenile voice, and, of course, his language was quite improper, and what he said was simply nonsense, yet those around me *howled,* as though these were the pearls of Oscar Wilde being thrown before them. Unutterably fascinating! I wanted you to be there, Lili, to assure me I had not *lost* my mind.

Lili Uh-huh.

Eva Everyone asked after you at dinner—aren't you hungry, why aren't you eating? Olivia has prepared for us a lovely porridge. (*Lili takes a bite.*) That's good. At any rate, I had a pencil with me, my little gold pencil, and I recorded my impressions of the event on a cocktail napkin, lest I forget them. What an extraordinary evening. Yet, not at all . . . untypical . . . for the region. Ve-e-e-ry strange.

Olivia Would you like me to make something else, Lili?

Lili No.

Eva That darling Mindy Kahkstein was there. A *m-o-ost* peculiar girl. One of those American girls who can't seem to get used to their bosoms. To show or not to show. To slump or stand erect. You feel these are her sole concerns. She asked after you.

Olivia Would you like milk instead of coffee, Lili? I'll get you some.

Lili Coffee's fine.

Eva And, of course, I spent time with Libby Kahkstein—a woman who is *tres cher,* but not, I think, intellectually robust. And, once again, she disgraced herself at table. Why, when I tell you what she ate, and in what quantities! The *salad*—served at the beginning—barbaric, anyway, but Libby tore into it like a savage woman. And the Russian dressing—not just a dollop, either, but *gobules*— Gobules? . . . —*Globules*. Then the consomme, then the derma, smothered in gravy and onions, then the filet mignon—a steak the size and shape of a jackboot also smothered in gravy. With a vast baked potato, into which Libby Kahkstein scooped not merely sour cream and chives, but five pats of butter. *Plus* asparagus with hollandaise. *Plus*—infinite numbers of buttered rolls, with seeds popping everywhere. *Plus* sherbet between courses. *Plus,* barrels of cream soda. *Plus*—coffee with heavy cream and parfait. Then—*then*—after the meal was over, and there was a little desultory dancing—out came this enormous Viennese Table. And Libby Kahkstein—using every ounce of energy available to her simply to transport her laden bulk—helped herself not *once,* not *twice,* but *three* times. To Napoleon, Sacher Torte, and a large plate of little cookies. *Incroyable!* But, my darling, why aren't you eating your breakfast?

Lili I don't know.

Eva You must . . . you must keep up your strength. Next time, you will come with me. It will please me to have you by my side, just for your humorous way of looking at things.

Lili I don't want to go.

Olivia I'll make you some dry toast.

Lili I'm perfectly all right. Please leave me alone. (*Beat.*)

Eva Now, Lili, we are only trying our best—

Olivia It's all right.

Eva —our very best to help you, my darling—

Olivia Nobody ever died from missing breakfast.

Eva And if we misspeak ourselves sometimes, that's—

Lili I don't need anything. Thank you. And I'd rather not be asked. (*Beat.*)

Eva Well, then, my darling, you shan't be. (*Beat.*)

Lili Thank you. (*They sit quietly a moment. Eva and Olivia resume eating.*)

Eva But . . . you must . . . Lili, you must come *out* a bit—

Lili Why?

Eva For your health.

Lili My health is fine.

Eva For your *well-being.* (*Beat.*) It is something all the doctors have agreed upon. All we are here for—all we want—Olivia and I—is for our girl to be happy again.

Lili I am.

Eva Yes?

Lili (*Sullen.*) Drunk with it. (*Beat.*)

Eva Well, at any rate, I am pleased that you have not entirely confined your circle of acquaintances to us two old ladies—

Lili What do you mean?

Eva Nothing, nothing—

Lili What do you mean?

Eva ... Merely that Olivia informs me she has seen you—on more than one occasion, I believe—in the company of a most attractive young man from across the lake.

Lili Olivia should be shot between the eyes.

Eva Lili! (*Olivia starts laughing.*) What a thing to say! All I meant was I am terribly *pleased*.

Lili And then her corpse should be thrown to sharks—

Eva My darling, no!

Olivia She doesn't mean it.

Lili Every word. (*Pause. Lili stares balefully at Olivia; Olivia looks back; her good-humor gives way. Eva sighs.*)

Eva Another one of these breakfasts. (*Beat.*) My darling, my sweetheart . . . (*To Olivia.*) My maid. (*Beat.*) I shall leave you to sort yourselves out. Now I must go and lie in the bathtub to soak for two hours in salted water. The price I must pay for the sins of a corrupt and sporting youth. (*Eva exits. Olivia and Lili are left alone, separate and sullen. After a long silence, Lili goes over to Olivia and embraces her.*)

Olivia (*Yielding gruffly.*) Oh, sure, sure, yes, now you want to be friends.

Lili I don't really think your corpse should be thrown to the sharks.

Olivia Generous of you. Why do you treat your mother like you do?

Lili How do I treat her?

Olivia Like you do.

Lili She used to sing, "The Nazis haven't found us, but darling they're around us." I was in my crib.

Olivia You were born difficult. A difficult girl.

Lili I'm a breeze.

Olivia Ho-ho!

Lili What?

Olivia You used to run away—

Lili I was a child—

Olivia We'd find you in the basement with the mailman, sorting letters. We'd find you on Broadway in a coffee shop, drinking coffee black—

Lili I liked the way it ate my stomach out—

Olivia Or we'd find you not at all, you'd just show up.

Lili I came back to you—I missed your lap . . . I used to think you were Buddha.

Olivia Hush.

Lili I'd chant, shantih, shantih, shantih, I want to die!

Olivia Enough of that kind of talk.

Lili April is the cruelest month . . .

Olivia This is July. A balmy July.

Lili This was then . . . when I was a child.

Olivia You were no picnic.

Lili Wasn't I a picnic?

Olivia Your mother was a woman alone. She gave you nice things. Good schools. She made her way. That was not easy, not easy at all—

Lili Is she still sick?

Olivia She's climbing her way out.

Lili I'll be better. I'll be kind.

Olivia She says she doesn't want you to bother—she says you're young—

Lili (*Chuckling grimly.*) The witch . . .

Olivia Lili!

Lili Olivia, how old are you when it's too late to start being happy?

Olivia Thirty-five.

Lili Oh, I have time . . .

Olivia (*Noting her distraction.*) Who are you *looking* for?

Lili . . . No one.

Olivia That boy?

Lili He's a man, he has a criminal record.

Olivia He *what*?

Lili I made that up.

Olivia Why?

Lili It came to me.

Olivia You shouldn't speak off the top of your head.

Lili I like the top of my head.

Olivia It will get you into trouble someday.

Lili I hope so. Did you have a ravenous sex life we know nothing about?

Olivia Lili . . .

Lili I'd respect you for it, I wouldn't call you a slut . . .

Olivia Lili . . .

Lili Are you a virgin?

Olivia Lili . . .

Lili You could be either of these things. I don't know you at all.

Olivia Being known is not part of my job . . .

Lili Olivia, does your knitting ever become anything? Or do you unravel it every night? Are you stalling until your husband comes back from the wars?

Olivia I'm going into town later to buy food. Is there anything special you want for dinner?

Lili What did my father die of? (*Beat.*)

Olivia Pneumonia.

Lili I thought it was malaria.

Olivia Well, maybe it was.

Lili Was he in Panama or something? Who dies of malaria on Central Park West?

Olivia You ask and ask and ask. What are you planning to do with all these answers if you get them?

Lili Make them into belts.

Olivia Difficult. A difficult girl. (*Looking out.*) There's that young man.

Lili . . . Where?

Olivia Over there . . . with that girl, that Mindy girl.

Lili Oh. (*Beat.*) That's a bagatelle. We're best friends already.

Olivia Do you even know him? . . . Who is he?

Lili His name is Nicky Lockridge.

Olivia Oh, Nicky Lockridge.

Lili And he's a Prince . . . from the east . . .

Olivia A bedtime story.

Lili Yes. A bedtime story. (*She curls up by Olivia's legs.*) On his piebald steed—I like that word, piebald—

Olivia It's a good word—

Lili He charges the fields of Greenwich and Darien. His life is a round of jousts and tourneys and tennis matches and he's a mean man with a La Crosse stick. His family's heraldic crest is centuries old, and yet this young prince is sore at heart—

Olivia Sore at heart—

Lili Yes, sore at heart. For to whom can he dedicate his jousts and tourneys? To what fair maiden can he offer the bull's ear?—He's a matador, too.

Olivia Right, right—on *weekends*.

Lili So he's plunged himself into a journey of matrimonial intent. Fearlessly, he's scaled the mighty Catskills. Fearlessly, he's met the natives of darkest Kiamesha, and he has conquered. He has conquered. The pennants shiver in the wind; the maypole drops its streamers. For Nicky has met his match. (*Offstage, Eva begins to hum the lullaby, "Nicht ist das gluck. . . ." Lili reacts to it almost as though physically striken. She closes her eyes and listens, motionless. Olivia comes behind her and holds her. They stay this way until Eva finishes.*) Olivia, I'm getting married. Nicky's asked me to marry him.

Olivia Lili!

Lili Don't breathe a word . . . (*She exits sharply.*)

Fade Out. End of Scene.

SCENE THREE. *Lili lies in the hammock, listening to Bobby Darin sing, "Beyond the Sea"* * on her transistor radio. Nick enters.*

Lili Bobby Darin.

Nick I know.

Lili I am not the praying sort, but if I were—I would leave this hammock and genuflect to Bobby Darin. I wait all afternoon for Bobby Darin to come on the radio.

Nick He's a good singer.

Lili Are you the praying sort?

Nick No, can't say that I am, not very much, no. (*Lili flicks off transistor radio.*)

Lili So, Nick, long time no see. What brings you here?

Nick You told Mindy I had clap. (*Beat.*)

Lili No, she got it wrong. What I said was, when I see you pass, you're such a sterling figure, it makes me *want* to clap. It got lost in translation. From English to Mindy.

Nick It's like a goddamn whispering gallery over there. Suddenly I'm getting the most incredible looks.

Lili I have no idea what you're talking about.

Nick I do not appreciate being associated with a venereal disease. It's not anything I can capitalize on.

* See Special Note on copyright page.

Lili I have no idea what you're talking about . . .

Nick Lili! (*Beat. She looks at him.*) Stop lying . . . Please, please stop lying. (*Beat.*)

Lili Why did you stop coming around?

Nick I got . . . busy.

Lili Oh, yes? *Time* dispatched you to Southeast Asia, did it?

Nick Busy here.

Lili There is no such thing as busy here—

Nick There was a . . .

Lili What?

Nick Shuffleboard tournament.

Lili Ah!

Nick . . . I won.

Lili It only adds more luster. (*Beat.*)

Nick I have obligations, you know. Other . . . obligations. To the people I'm here with. They *brought* me here.

Lili So?

Nick So . . . it's . . . it's incumbent upon me to spend time with them.

Lili Why?

Nick Why? Why do you keep asking me why? It's practically pre-moral of you.

Lili Pre-moral—does that come by way of Mindy, the Psychology Major?

Nick Education.

Lili Education, yes, I forgot.

Nick No . . . it doesn't come by way of Mindy. It's . . . it's just the code.

Lili I'll go across the lake for you now, Nicky. I'll go and apologize to Mindy, and tell her it was all a ghastly mistake. One of my capricious jokes. They all think I'm crazy, anyway.

Nick She's gone.

Lili . . . No!

Nick The whole family—

Lili When?

Nick About an hour ago.

Lili . . . Why?

Nick Mr. Kahkstein heard the rumor. (*Beat.*)

Lili I'm sorry.

Nick It seems you're a very persuasive storyteller. It seems Mindy returned to their cabana in tears.

Lili Oh God, no . . .

Nick Mrs. Kahkstein asked her why she was crying—

Lili She didn't—

Nick She's not as circumspect as other girls I've known—

Lili She's a cow—

Nick Please don't. I am involved, you know that.

Lili Yes, I'm sorry, again, I'm sorry—

Nick Mrs. Kahkstein turned out to be more pragmatic than I'd anticipated. She said, "Well, darling, men can be that way. At least you found out in time."

Lili Oh, no . . .

Nick Well, at that, Mindy cried even harder and Mrs. Kahkstein said, "Mindy—if this is true—it doesn't affect *you*, does
it?"

Lili She told the truth?

Nick She said, "Yes, mother it does. We've slept together.
Over and over and over again."

Lili The fool—

Nick Mr. Kahkstein apparently purpled at this and swore
he'd have my scalp—

Lili I'll tell them, I'll call, I'll alert the Coast Guard—

Nick He said, something like, "That . . ." *gondiff*?

Lili Gonniff—it means thief—

Nick Yes, well, he said, "That gonniff, I'll see him dead for
taking my daughter's virtue and giving her a disease."

Lili He could do it, too. New Jersey is lousy with Cosa
Nostra, I'm sure he has connections—

Nick But then, *Mindy*—who was not at her best—said,
"Daddy, don't be ridiculous. He didn't take my virtue. I've
slept with hundreds of men. I'm afraid I gave it to *him*."

Lili Even I gave her more credit than—

Nick Well, he didn't know *what* to do when he heard this, so
he punched the wall, yelled at his wife, and ended up giving
me a cigar. Would you like it? It's Havana. Before the revolu-
tion. Which, I think, must make it more a souvenir than a
smoke.

Lili I'm evil.

Nick You're . . . effective.

Lili Well, what should I do, Nick? Should I write a letter?

Nick Oh, who knows? I don't understand how anyone's mind works any more. For all I know, everything will be fine in the morning, and we'll still be engaged.

Lili (*Startled.*) Engaged?

Nick . . . Yes.

Lili You never told me that part.

Nick It's new. . . . It's not official, it's . . . understood.

Lili (*Softly.*) You never told me.

Nick I know.

Lili We walked together. . . . Well, then, why are you here?

Nick I want to know why you did it.

Lili . . . I missed you.

Nick And this is the simplest way you could think of to deal with that problem?

Lili My mind doesn't run to simple ways . . . How is it you've been here so long, anyway? Don't you have a job to do? *Time* magazine must be incredibly liberal with its vacations. They ought to call it, "*Free* Time."

Nick Lili—

Lili Mindy has gone; why aren't you going too?

Nick The room still belongs to me and—

Lili That's not a reason—

Nick I want to see you.

Lili . . . Why?

Nick . . . I don't know anyone like you.

Lili Mindy's like me. Mindy's exactly like me. Except stupid and a cow.

Nick She isn't anything like you.

Lili —and a raving, famous nymphomaniac.

Nick Granted.

Lili I'll be a raving, famous nymphomaniac, maybe, some-day—

Nick That's not an ambition.

Lili Did my mother give you money to stop seeing me? (*Beat.*)

Nick You shouldn't have said that . . .

Lili I'm sorry, I'm sorry—but it's something she'd try—

Nick The last time I saw you, you ran in the other direction because you were with her.

Lili You can't meet her.

Nick God! Why can't you just relax?

Lili . . . Nick, I'm rich all by myself. Next year I get all this money my father left me. And there's nothing she can do about it.

Nick Money couldn't have less to do with anything.

Lili . . . Because sex is the only currency that matters when you're my age.

Nick I'm sorry, but you're a little . . . *warped* . . . where some things are concerned.

Lili So I have been repeatedly told. (*Beat.*) Oh, you know too much about me. Why can't we talk about you once in a while instead? Tell me something . . .

Nick Like what?

Lili Anything terrible. (*Beat.*)

Nick . . . You already said nothing ever happened to me.

Lili I said that's what you look like.

Nick Maybe I'm afraid it's true.

Lili But I want it to be true. I want you to have been spared *everything.* (*Pause. He is brought up short by the sincerity of this.*)

Nick (*A concession.*) I stopped seeing you because Mindy asked me to.

Lili . . . Why?

Nick Because you're beautiful.

Lili That can't be pos—

Nick Accept it. (*Pause.*)

Lili . . . Oh my God, I can't believe what I said to her. Awful, just awful.

Nick Yes.

Lili . . . It's just that you're such a surprise. . . . There was no preparing for you. . . . If I'd had a year or two, I might have been ready . . . (*Beat.*)

Nick Oh . . . look . . . why don't we *swim*?

Lili What?

Nick Let's swim. Let's just suit up and swim, Okay? And maybe have drinks after? I'm on vacation. I was hoping for a nice time.

Lili . . . I don't swim.

Nick What?

Lili I can't—I don't know how.

Nick That's terrible—How do you get through the day if you can't throw yourself into water? I'll teach you.

Lili You have to learn that sort of thing young.

Nick Listen, I can teach you the butterfly stroke in two weeks. By the end of the month, you'll be entering diving championships.

Lili I don't think I'd be able to—

Nick I learned pinochle with Moe Kahkstein: tit-for-tat—

Lili Of course you did. You're easy in all situations. Because when you're odd man out, everyone else feels uncomfortable —It's the gift of your hegemony . . .

Nick All these words! (*Beat.*)

Lili What are you offering, really? (*Olivia enters.*)

Olivia Lili, we're having tea.

Lili I'm with someone, Olivia.

Olivia I've set four places.

Lili . . . No.

Olivia Your mother says, she's looking forward to meeting the young man, after all this time. Will you join us, Mr.—

Nick Nick Lockridge.

Olivia Will you join us, Mr. Lockridge?

Nick I'll be very happy to—

Lili But—

Nick Lead the way . . . (*Olivia and Nick start off. Lili holds back a moment.*)

Lili . . . To lose you to her so soon. (*She starts off after them.*)

Fade Out. End of Scene.

SCENE FOUR. *Eva and Nick at tea table. Olivia presides. Lili idles, paces, leans on the periphery.*

Olivia More tea, Mr. Lockridge?

Nick Yes, please. It's wonderful tea.

Eva Another biscuit?

Nick Thank you.

Eva Have you spent much time in the mountains?

Nick Winters, mostly . . .

Eva Ah, yes, winters . . . I suspect you of being deeply and confirmedly aquatic.

Nick Very much so.

Eva Yes, yes. . . . Personally, I don't trust the sea. I do not even, if such a thing is not unutterably foolish, I do not *approve* of the sea—

Nick (*Smiling.*) Really?

Lili It's a mania—

Eva No, I feel that illusion of limitlessness . . . that challenge to embark . . . to sail . . . to immerse oneself in an element for which one is not naturally, not physiologically equipped. . . . These things I believe to be seductive and subversive and tragic—

Nick Huh!

Eva In the mountains, on the other hand—the borders are visible, tangible, and *everywhere*. Very trustworthy.

Nick I guess I never looked at it that way before.

Eva It is for this reason that we come here year after year. Though it means we must suffer proximity to some of this country's most comical misfits. But even that is a good thing

—it is good to stay in touch with the lower life forms. Olivia tells me you wish to be an architect—

Nick Olivia?

Lili Olivia!

Eva I love architects. Has Lili told you yet of my affair with Mies van der Rohe?

Nick No—no, she hasn't—

Eva She will get to it. Of course, it's a preposterous idea, but it's a thing she likes to say.

Lili It came on the heels of her affair with Himmler.

Eva (*Gaily.*) Yes, my darling, spin, spin . . . (*Smiles conspiratorially at Nick.*) Now what kind of architect do you wish to be?

Nick Every kind.

Eva Yes, I'd forgotten. There is never any need to ask an American this sort of question; one always receives the same answer. And what do you wish to build?

Nick A whole city.

Eva Do you mean, by that, that you wish to build an entire city yourself or that you wish to build a city that is technologically integrated, spiritually complete, and well-managed?

Nick The latter.

Lili All the cities have already been built.

Nick Not all of them.

Eva So. . . . As one who is interested in these things, what is your opinion of my little *Nicht Ahin, Nicht Ahier*? (*Beat.*)

Nick I'm sorry . . . I don't understand the question. Is that German?

Eva In a manner of speaking. *Nicht Ahin, Nicht Ahier* is my little name for our house—Because it belongs neither to the hotel nor to the little rural outposts on this side of the lake. But I am being foolish—the house is humble and not for criticism. A whole city—my, my! Now, tell me, where did you study architecture? Where did you get your degree?

Nick I haven't . . . actually . . . yet.

Eva You haven't? . . . But you are not so very young, are you?

Nick No—not so very young.

Eva But who am I to talk? I saw Methuselah in his pram—why have you not studied yet?

Nick . . . I was going to start a couple of years ago . . . but things got in the way—

Eva Things?

Nick Personal things—

Eva Too personal to share, I understand—

Nick No, no—

Eva Nothing is required of you—

Nick Oh, that's really—

Eva We make a point never to pry—

Nick My father died a while ago and I've been . . . sidetracked.

Eva (*Gently.*) . . . Oh my dear. . . . How did he die? May I ask it?

Nick Stupidly. . . . It was a freak accident. He was cleaning his gun . . . and it went off . . .

Lili Nicky . . .

Eva I am so terribly, terribly sorry . . .

Nick It was tough at first, but I guess I'm used to it, now—

Eva And your mother?

Nick My mother died the year before.

Eva Oh, my dear, random things, random things . . .

Nick Yes . . . random.

Eva But it is the people to whom random things happen, and who are then able to survive, flourish . . . it is these people who will see Damascus. My husband and I were in Germany until the last possible moment. We were to discover that the boat we took was the last boat out. What would have happened if we had missed the boat . . . (*Lili has begun to skip rope.*)

Olivia Lili—

Eva Oh, look, Lili has decided to entertain us with a sporting event—There, my dear, skip, skip, don't mind us . . .

Lili It's wonderful exercise. Prize fighters do it.

Eva Just think of the shock for me, Mr. Lockridge—all my background, all my education, and I have given birth to Sonny Liston—

Lili Nicky and Lili up a tree—

Eva We are not an eccentric family, Nicky—

Lili K.I.S.S.I.N.G.

Eva Just a little giddy around the circumference—

Lili First comes love/Then comes marriage—

Nick Lili!

Eva Have you discussed this scenario, or is Lili improvising?

Lili Then comes Nicky with the baby carriage—

Nick That's very embarrassing—

Eva My daughter is this way because her father indulged her; he found her irresistible—

Nick What was it Mr. Adler did?

Lili My father invented teflon—

Eva Mr. Adler invented—

Lili He invented Bakelite—

Eva He had the patent on—

Lili He blazed the trail for macaroni-and-cheese—

Eva Mr. Adler's work was in—

Lili He invented the reversible condom—

Eva (*Gently.*) Lili . . . (*Beat.*)

Lili (*Softly; chastened.*) Something in lamps. He invented something that's in lamps . . . something that's in lamps; excuse me, please . . . (*She exits quickly.*)

Nick Lili—(*But she's gone.*) I should go after her.

Eva No, please stay with me. Olivia will see to her. . . . Will you, please, Olivia?

Olivia Of course.

Eva Follow at a good distance, remember . . . (*Olivia exits.*) Lili has gone through many corrections, but she retains her genius for the inappropriate.

Nick What upsets her so much?

Eva Oh, my daughter, my darling daughter. . . . Inside her head is a sort of masked ball; you never know with whom you are dancing. . . . You seem fond of Lili.

Nick I am.

Eva Genuinely fond. . . . Oh, it is always so hard, this part . . . Lili is not charmingly eccentric. She is not your garden variety neurotic. She's been hospitalized.

Nick Why?

Eva Who knows, who knows? *This* is better than usual.

Nick But how long has she been this way? When did it start?

Eva Oh, it began before it ever began. Has Lili ever told you that I murdered her father?

Nick . . . No.

Eva Obviously, that means, yes. . . . Yes. Well, I think she half-believes it, you know. And who can blame her? After the thing that happened to Mr. Adler, there was no consoling anyone in that house.

Nick What happened to him?

Eva Everything in the world. And nothing you could possibly understand . . . I loved my husband for subtle reasons and he was annihilated for a crude one. . . . But that is no kind of story for a summer night. . . . Oh, my dear, how can you take the sadness away from a girl who learned it so early in life? It is not possible. It can't be done. Every summer we come here and there's someone. Some sweet boy from across the lake. We hope, we pray but it's no good. Nothing has worked. It always ends in disaster.

Nick Are you trying to scare me off?

Eva Are you scared?

Nick Not at all. (*Beat.*)

Eva Oh, no, no, no. . . . That is not it at all . . . I simply wonder what kind of effect you might have on her? To pay attention, to flatter her with your presence, when you have, after all, a life you must return to, responsibilities—

Nick There's nothing that pressing—

Eva Oh, but surely . . . they require you back at . . . *Time,* is it?

Nick Not for a while, no. (*Beat.*)

Eva But, then, in New York and . . . Darien, did you say?

Nick Yes, Darien . . .

Eva Yes, Darien . . . aren't there people who are missing you?

Nick No one that I care to see. (*Eva looks at him quizzically.*) No one I need to see right away. (*Beat.*)

Eva Well . . . yes, then . . . yes. . . . Perhaps this would be just the thing. Perhaps you are what we have waited for.

Nick She thinks . . . I shouldn't say this—

Eva Tell me.

Nick . . . She thinks you want to keep me away from her.

Eva She thinks I am the opposite of what I am . . . Will you tell her, my dear? Will you tell her that I have not discouraged you? That I wish what she does? And will you be good to her? Whatever the cost? (*Beat.*)

Nick The cost?

Eva Do you smell rain? I must take off my rings; my joints will swell. (*She removes her rings; they fall to the ground.*) Oh, how clumsy I am!

Nick Here let me—(*Nick kneels to search for them.*)

Eva No, don't bother, it's too dark—you'll never find them.

Nick But they're diamonds!

Eva They will be there in the morning.

Nick But what if they're not?

Eva Then they're not. (*Slowly he rises, faces her.*) Whatever you can do, my dear. That may not be much. After all, we can't expect miracles. (*They look at each other.*)

   Fade Out. End of Scene.

SCENE FIVE. *Lili alone. Nick enters.*

Lili The hospital was her idea.

Nick What?

Lili I wasn't really sick. I was fine. She didn't think so. On my twenty-first birthday I get the money my father left me. Then I'll be well.

Nick All right. (*Beat.*)

Lili So she did tell you?

Nick Yes.

Lili Of course. So you'll leave me.

Nick She doesn't want me to leave; she asked me not to.

Lili That way when you do she'll seem blameless ... It's one of her oldest tricks.

Nick Lili—

Lili Why did you tell her all those things you never told me?

Nick ... She draws it out ...

Lili She has you now.

Nick It's not that complicated.

Lili This happens all the time. We come here every year: "Please, Lili, play," she says. "Be happy, be free. Please, Lili, find someone and don't frighten him away—" I frighten everyone—

Nick You don't frighten me—

Lili She'll do that for me—

Nick No—

Lili Oh, trust me—

Nick Don't—

Lili Why don't you just go away now? Why don't you just leave me alone?

Nick Why are you going on like this?

Lili Because I love you. (*Beat; simply.*) I know that sounds crazy, but I'm not crazy—I know my own name—I don't see things—and I love you . . . I know I can't ever have you, I know I lie . . . I do awful things . . . I don't know why . . . I can't explain it . . . I feel as if everything I've ever done was something that happened *to* me. . . . That sounds crazy, too. . . . Oh God, this isn't making you think any better of me . . . I'm sorry . . . I haven't meant anything. . . . Just go . . . (*Beat.*)

Nick Nothing you said sounds crazy—No, *listen.* . . . Nothing you said sounds crazy. And I don't believe you've ever done anything so terrible. You have this way of seeing yourself—I think it just comes from living in dark rooms with bad air—Listen—all this stuff about what you've done—even if you *have* done it—Pasts are . . . they're nothing. . . . Things can be so much simpler . . .

Lili Look—she'll probably be here soon—It would be better if you just—

Nick Forget her! . . . The hell with her. . . . There are some people we have to pretend don't exist. . . . We just have to forget about—no matter how it hurts. . . . Some people we just have to get away from—

Lili I can't do that.

Nick I know you can.

Lili You don't understand.

Nick I do.

Lili She's what I have . . . (*Pause.*)

Nick When we met . . . it wasn't the first time I'd seen you . . . I'd been watching you . . . I came here for you . . . I came here to meet you—

Lili You said—

Nick I lied.

Lili But—

Nick Don't talk! . . . And ever since then, I've been. . . . Look, it wasn't because of Mindy that I stopped seeing you. I was scared . . . because I'd never wanted anything so much. (*Beat.*)

Lili That can't be possible.

Nick Why not? . . . Because you want it to be?

Lili . . . Yes.

Nick Then maybe your luck has changed. (*Beat.*)

Lili . . . But will you be on my side? Whatever happens . . . will you be on my side? (*He kisses her.*) Nick—?

Nick What?

Lili Let's swim. (*They kiss again and lie down. "Beyond the Sea"* * *plays.*)

 Fade Out. End of Scene.

---

* See Special Note on copyright page.

SCENE SIX. *Nick and Eva alone. Eva is using a cane.*

Eva It has warmed my heart to see the change in Lili over these last weeks.

Nick We've been very happy. She's swimming now.

Eva Swimming, my God, what a wonder you are!

Nick I don't take credit. . . . The cane . . .

Eva Yes.

Nick I've never seen it before.

Eva Ah, well—the body is weak, the body is strong, everything is reversible. Where shall we have the wedding, here do you think, or in town?

Nick I think that should be up to Lili. I think that would be best.

Eva What a kind young man you are, how considerate. (*Beat.*) Now, let me tell you what I have discovered about you.

Nick Excuse me?

Eva First, you do not work for *Time*.

Nick What are you talking about?

Eva One does not find you on their employee roster. Or on any Luce publication—or any publication at all, for that matter.

Nick I can show you my press card.

Eva Does it have an expiration date?

Nick No.

Eva Too bad. Defunct things should declare themselves defunct. You were fired several months ago. . . . You do not remonstrate. Good. This will go smoothly, then.

Nick I—

Eva Ah-ah . . . don't interrupt my flow. Second, you have no money whatsoever. I have researched your family—given a certain amount of money, one does have contacts, you know, even against one's will. You come from one of those fine blood-edifices that started to crumble virtually upon erection. A fortune with perhaps a crime attached to it. Social registry. Neglect—sudden bankruptcy—a very American story, very boring.

Nick Eva, listen—

Eva Third—and most regrettably—your father did not die in a freak accident while cleaning his gun—

Nick I'm afraid you're wrong there—

Eva Well, then he must have been licking it clean for the bullet discharged in his mouth. (*Beat.*) Ah. I am sorry for you for this part. (*Beat.*) After that, you lost your job and started to wander. Apparently, you fell quite off the edge of the universe. The rumors had it you were with distant relatives—or friends of friends—here for a week—there for a month—however you people disport yourselves. A mode of existence that must have been unsettling for you—to say nothing of frugal. Then you discovered the girl who brought you here—This part is puzzling. . . . Surely, there's some lovely girl of your own kind who would have found in you an excellent candidate for renovation, and drawn you back into the fold—oh, yes, that seems a much more likely scenario than carpet heiresses and the Catskills, no? Well, never mind. Finally, you arrived here and met my daughter, and proceeded to tell not a single true thing about yourself. Yes, I believe that brings us up to date with you. (*Beat.*) Now. Is there anything you'd like to say?

Nick (*Very quietly.*) I don't think so.

Eva I think perhaps you should. I think it's an opportunity you shouldn't pass up. (*Long pause. When Nick finally speaks, it's with a simplicity meant to control the difficulty of what he's saying.*)

Nick After my mother died, my father more-or-less lost control of things. Not badly—it was more a kind of slip of attention. But, apparently, that's all it took. Things fell apart. It had something to do with a partner, I think, or the board—something shifty—I'm not suppressing the details here, I just never quite learned them. Anyway, just like that, it seemed, we were out of business. Suddenly, as you said. And, yes, broke. I was working in New York then, I'd visit on week-ends. Every time I did, he'd have sold off another room of furniture and he'd be sitting in it . . . singing. "I'm a ramblin' wreck from Georgia Tech/And a heck of an engineer . . ." And he wasn't even drinking—that was the funny part, he was stone-cold sober. I'd say, "Dad . . . are you sure you're all right? Can I get you anything?" He'd say, "Oh, no, I'm fine, pal, I'm fine, sport—all I need is a shave and a haircut—that's all I need, sport—a shave and a haircut—just a shave and a haircut—then I'll be ready." (*Beat.*) He didn't understand how everything had happened to him so fast. He wasn't crazy, I don't think . . . just surprised. . . . He started singing in the street. He'd forget to *bathe*. The house started looking like a junkheap. One day this group of men—five of them, I think . . . our neighbors . . . came to call on him. They said to him, "Nick, we're sorry to have to say this, but it doesn't look as if you're ever going to be able to take control of things. Wouldn't it be better to go, now, before you have to? Wouldn't it be better just to leave?" (*Beat.*) He called me in the city after. I said, "Oh, look, they're your friends, they'll forget about it." He said, "No . . . I stank up the street. You can do a lot of things, but you don't stink up the street." And he started to laugh. We hung up, he walked into his room . . . and had the unfortunate accident while cleaning his gun. (*Beat.*) I didn't tell any of this to Lili because, well, it isn't the sort of thing

130

you say right at first . . . and because it was so pleasant not to. Those are the only reasons. (*Beat.*) Well. This has been a marvelous party, you've been a perfect hostess, and I've had a splendid time. (*Beat.*) I wish you would let me tell Lili instead of you.

Eva Oh, but I have no intention of telling her.

Nick . . . Then what are you going to do?

Eva After you marry, I will pay for your graduate school in architecture, then give you a start in business.

Nick . . . What?

Eva There—you made me give it away—that was meant to be my surprise.

Nick I can take care of all that myself.

Eva You mean with Lili's money. No, you see, this is where you are wrong. Has Lili told you she comes into her money on her twenty-first birthday? Yes; this is a thing she says. In truth, she does come into money. On her thirty-fifth birthday. Until then, it is only what she earns or what I give her. Now, tell me, what are your plans for getting through school and life? Go moment by moment. (*Beat.*) Yes, I will pay for you gladly for we will be related.

Nick . . . That isn't right, somehow . . .

Eva You have a conscience, excellent! I'll write that down. Oh, look! To deny happiness because it looks like something it is not. . . . You have told me everything about yourself— now I understand and pity you. You love my daughter—you are in a condition I can remedy—what stupidity—what *cruelty*—not to let me. (*Beat.*)

Nick Then I'll tell her about this.

Eva That I cannot allow.

Nick . . . What?

Eva If you will tell her, she will tell me; if she will tell me, I will renege.

Nick Why?

Eva Do you know how this will look to her? This lie and that lie. A few swimming lessons do not make one psychologically whole, I'm sorry if you thought that was the case. We don't want to risk your losing her affection, do we?

Nick But—

Eva Figure nothing out; look no further; all is well.

Nick I don't understand. Why don't you just tell her everything and be rid of me?

Eva Because there isn't very much we can hope for Lili, but at least we can hope for the best.

Nick And what is the best, do you think?

Eva An intricately unhappy life, I'm afraid, lived out in compensatory splendor.

Nick I don't believe that! (*Beat.*)

Eva And why not?

Nick (*Pulling back a little.*) . . . I cause happiness; that's what I do. (*Beat.*)

Eva How nice for you! Well—I believe I must go in—everything aches.

Nick Eva—!

Eva What?

Nick I really do love her, you know.

Eva That is no longer either here or there.

Fade Out. End Act I.

Act Two

SCENE ONE. *Eva and Olivia. A table set for tea.*

Eva Oh, Olivia, this dampness is terrible, every bone in my body aches. (*Olivia lights a cigarette.*) That is an awful habit.

Olivia (*Gleefully.*) Yes.

Eva What do you have for us this afternoon? Is it scrumptious, is it special?

Olivia See for yourself. (*Tilts a cake from the table towards her.*)

Eva (*Mildly disdainful.*) . . . Yes. Well . . .

Olivia You're in a mood.

Eva Mmm. . . . Have I told you of *shneckens*? And *hörnchen*? With real whipped cream?

Olivia Often.

Eva . . . Yes. Well, I miss them. It is to be tea, I suppose.

Olivia Always tea.

Eva I long for demitasse.

Olivia I can do that.

Eva But the spoons, the spoons, the *macher* spoons—They are somewhere in a basement in Cologne. . . . How can you have demitasse when the spoons are elsewhere?

Olivia Huh!

Eva Some nights my dreams are filled with tiny spoons . . . and *shnecken* and *hörnchen* . . .

Olivia You come through a war and grieve for the lost whipped cream—I won't figure it out.

Eva And what do you miss and what do you long for? (*Olivia smiles.*) You are a Sphinx, there is no getting it out of you. Aren't there nights when you are lonely and long to tell someone something?

Olivia Yes. But if I did, I think I'd end up lonelier for the information I'd given away.

Eva . . . Hm. Yes . . . (*Beat.*) I am hearing him again.

Olivia Mr. Adler . . .

Eva . . . Walking up and down the hallway, hour after hour . . .

Olivia Those were bad years.

Eva The years in which someone tries to die always are. . . . They killed him. As if with a knife. As if with a gun.

Olivia So you say . . .

Eva What else can you call it? To do that to a genius . . .

Olivia I never understood all that business; I never knew why they did that to Mr. Adler . . .

Eva Do you remember the joke, "After the war the Jews were so popular they were trying to get their old noses back?"

Olivia Yes.

Eva It was a joke. (*Beat.*) Oh, they were so discreet, so tactful. They said to him, "Yes, we will manufacture your invention. Sign the contract and you will have everything in the world." We were so happy, we celebrated. Then—three weeks? A month. They told him, "This can be an enormous thing, a breakthrough! But we must not give way to sentimentality. You must see that Walter Parson—(the partner he had taken on who had done virtually nothing)—Walter Parson with his smooth voice and his smooth history—you must see that he is the better man for all this—For the conventions and the advertisements, for the conferences and the symposia. This is a time of plenty," they said, "Not of sad faces with leaky eyes. Oh, but why do you protest? We give you all the money in the world and all you have to do is disappear a little . . ." These men . . . these men who come with their generous offers to take away everything you possess. . . . But why do you stare at me?

Olivia I like that boy, that Nick.

Eva Do you? And you are such a shrewd judge of character. Tell me—why do you like him?

Olivia Because Lili does.

Eva And do you think he loves her?

Olivia I have no reason to believe otherwise . . .

Eva But does it seem *likely*?

Olivia Anything that's already happened is likely—that's my opinion.

Eva Yes. . . . Oh, but, Olivia, I fully agree—I was *testing* you! Have I been in anyway discouraging?

Olivia Not yet.

Eva Then relax. (*Olivia keeps looking at her.*) Oh, I am stiff again . . . please? I would appreciate it. (*Olivia puts out her cigarette, rubs Eva's shoulders.*) You are wonderful at this. I love you dearly.

Olivia Oh, don't.

Eva Then I won't. See how amenable I am? It is a quality in myself I am surprised is so seldom remarked.

Olivia I don't believe I've ever heard anyone mention it.

Eva People miss the point, don't you think?

Olivia I don't know any people. (*Gil enters.*)

Gil Goddamn, would you look at this place!

Eva And what is this?

Gil Oh—hi—sorry—I didn't see you. I've been—I tell you it's been quite a time—but *this*—the view and the quiet. There's even furniture! . . . This is great . . .

Eva We like it. (*She looks to Olivia: Who is this person?*)

Gil I'll bet . . . I take it you're also fleeing the circus maximus over there?

Eva *Ah!*—you are with the hotel.

Gil For *two days*—

Eva You have my sympathy . . .

Gil Thank you. . . . It's just . . . well, I don't have to tell you. . . . Gals in cha-cha dresses—women in mink stoles in what month is this? . . . These *foods*—

Eva We mustn't speak of them!

Gil I came here—I thought I was going to *relax*—All of a sudden, I'm at these events, I'm doing the hokey-pokey, I'm winning sets of dishes in bingo games, I'm watching fifty-year-old women in chiffon dresses sing, "My Lord and Master" into a microphone, it's—Oh! There's this one guy, he calls himself a tumbler or something, as far as I can make out he's some type of social director—When I first got here I was allergic to the ragweed or something, every time I sneezed he'd say, "Stzeszetszt." What does that mean?

Eva Drop dead.

Gil Then I should stop thanking him. . . . This place though— You can read a book, you can take a nap, this is great. (*He lies down on the bench or somewhere, apparently intending to settle in for the duration.*)

Eva . . . And who are you, you enthusiastic and attractive young person?

Gil Sorry. Gil Harbison.

Eva I am Eva Adler, and this is Olivia Shaw.

Gil (*To Olivia.*) How do you do?

Olivia Do you have a twin?

Gil Excuse me?

Olivia I thought maybe you had a brother. Never mind. How do you do?

Gil Well, I'm just great, just great *now*. (*To Eva.*) Hey, are you the one the gals across the lake call the Czarina?

Eva If there is such a one, I would guess I am she.

Gil What a sentence—wonderful!—Americans never take grammar to that kind of extreme. I'm in publishing, I know this. They say you stay on this side of the lake a lot.

Eva This is my place.

Gil Really? . . . Wait. Am I trespassing?

Eva Yes.

Gil God—I'm sorry—I had no idea—This doesn't look like the sort of place someone *owns*.

Eva No, no, no. So tell me, is this your vacation?

Gil More-or-less. I was just looking for a change of scene.

Eva Was the old scene fatiguing you?

Gil I thought so—but *this* place—wow! Your little spot here, though—what an amazing relief. (*Notices tea service.*) Oh God, you're having tea—Well, then, I really should leave you alone. I don't want to interfere—by the way, that cake looks wonderful.

Olivia Thank you.

Gil Well, back to the third circle of Hell—

Eva Why don't you stay?

Gil Oh—no—

Eva Please—we're having a little celebration—the more the merrier—

Gil Thank you—that would be wonderful—

Olivia I'll bring another cup—or do you take it in a glass?

Gil Is it iced?

Olivia I'll bring a cup. (*Exits.*)

Eva Olivia is very witty when she's bored. Pay no attention.

Gil Whatever.

Eva Nick and Lili should be back any moment, now; then we'll have our tea.

Gil Nick and Lili?

Eva My daughter and her fiance. They've gone for a walk.

Gil Oh—oh right!

Eva What? The ladies by the lake told you about this, too?

Gil Well, you know. . . . Blabbety-blabbety . . .

Eva Are you here with anyone?

Gil No—I came just for the heck of it—

Eva I see. And how did you ever choose the Catskills?

Gil Well you know, after a while I got so bored with the East End and Nantucket and Fisher's and the Vineyard—I was looking for someplace I'd never been—and here it is—the Catskills.

Eva Two of you in one summer . . .

Gil I beg your pardon?

Eva Nothing, nothing at all. Oh, but here they are. (*Nick and Lili enter.*) How are you, my darlings? Look whom I have discovered—a fresh explorer.

Lili Hello.

Gil You're Lili, nice to meet you. I'm Gil Harbison.

Lili Nice to meet you.

Nick (*Extends his hand.*) Nick Lockridge; how do you do?

Gil You look familiar; have we met?

Nick I don't know; it's possible.

Eva Gil is at the hotel, too. I asked him to have tea with us.

Lili You *did*?

Eva Of course. Is that so surprising?

Lili Yes. (*Olivia enters with cup.*)

Eva My daughter thinks I am a hermit and an ogre—pay no attention. Where did you walk?

Lili Around the pool. People were asking about you.

Eva I am missed.

Lili I didn't say that. (*To Gil.*) Do you really think you've met before? I don't know anyone Nicky knows.

Gil Maybe. Were you at the Gold and Silver?

Nick Excuse me?

Gil The Gold and Silver Ball.

Nick What year?

Gil Fifty-five, fifty-six, fifty-seven, or fifty-eight, maybe? I went a lot.

Nick I don't remember.

Lili You don't remember fifty-five, fifty-six, fifty-seven, or fifty-eight?

Nick Maybe I was.

Lili Try to figure it out. I don't know anyone who knew you.

Eva Gil's in publishing.

Lili Really? Maybe that's how you know each other—Nicky writes for *Time*.

Gil No, it's book publishing.

Lili Really?

Gil I'm an editor at a small house—we're very sincere.

Lili How fun. What have you published?

Gil Nothing you'd have heard of. Right now, though, everybody there is on the lookout for a sexy, suburban novel—you know, "It lifts the lid off a small American town"—oh, I hope I haven't offended Olivia.

Olivia Of course not.

Gil I just thought you might be religious.

Olivia People think that.

Gil Anyway, I kind of regret that publishing's going in that direction. I find the older I get the more I respect people who are serious and the less I respect people who aren't.

Lili Nicky is extremely serious.

Nick Lili, please—

Lili He's going to go back to school and become an architect—

Gil Now architecture is something I can respect, that's a *field*—

Lili Nicky's going to become great at it—

Gil I'll bet.

Eva This is a policy of mine: Never doubt the young. Now, I must tell you all what the special treats are about. Nicky: This morning I called my accountant and he is going to set up that special fund for your education, plus another to start you off professionally, as we have discussed. He says there will be no problem at all.

Nick Eva—

Lili *What?* (*Beat. Nick stares at Eva, horrified.*)

Eva Oh, have I said something inopportune? Haven't you told her, Nicky? . . . Was I supposed to keep that to myself? I am old and often muddled these days. (*No one speaks. Lili looks to Nick, who does nothing.*)

Gil So, I think that's great that you're helping out, just great.

Eva Well, you know Nicky is part of the *mischpucha,* now.

Gil Part of the *what?* That doesn't sound like German.

Eva It's the only kind of German I speak these days. (*Lili has picked up the teapot and turned it over; tea trickles slowly onto the ground.*)

Olivia Lili!

Nick Lili, I—

Gil (*Overlapping.*) Is something going on? (*Lili, for the rest of the scene, is trying to beat back an overwhelming emotion—panic and confusion and hysteria. When she speaks, it's tense, clenched, her breathing shallow.*)

Lili I don't care—

141

Eva My darling, what have you done?

Lili I don't care if it's the money—it doesn't make any difference to me—

Nick Lili, please—

Lili I still want—I still want to be with you—I'll pay! I'll pay for everything!

Nick That isn't what this is—

Lili But did you—did you make a *deal* with her?

Nick Listen to me—

Lili Are you—are you on her side?

Nick No, listen—

Lili I'll pay for anything, but please—please—be on my side—

Eva My darling—

Nick Lili, come with me.

Lili *STOP!* I can't breathe! I can't breathe! (*She clutches herself tightly and her mouth opens as if she's about to scream, but only a strangulated sob comes out.*)

Nick Lili—(*She collapses.*)

   Blackout. End of Scene.

SCENE TWO. *Nick lies in the hammock. Gil is looking out at the lake.*

Gil I sat at the bar through last call. This woman in a grey beehive kept ordering Brandy Alexanders and trying to make me. I was sorely tempted.

Nick But you resisted.

Gil I was stalwart.

Nick You're an admirable young man.

Gil I think I am. People say so. (*Beat.*) So is tea always such an hysterical occasion here or was this special?

Nick No. This was special.

Gil I'm glad. . . . Is she okay?

Nick She's sleeping.

Gil She seems like a nice girl.

Nick I love her very much.

Gil I'm sure you do. . . . Why aren't you there?

Nick I've been banished.

Gil What?

Nick Yes. It seems I'm a dangerous influence. It seems I caused all that.

Gil My god!

Nick Eva's very clever, she covers her tracks. She said, "Consider where Lili sleeps the castle keep; consider Olivia the sentry."

Gil And what is she?

Nick (*German accent.*) I am the moat.

Gil What a night!

Nick Yeah.

Gil (*Looking out at lake.*) I had a hunch you'd be here. It's where I would be at this time of night. Just sort of swinging and swaying.

Nick Whatever. (*Gil moves to behind the hammock.*)

Gil It's so quiet . . . so dark. . . . A real country darkness.

Nick The hotel's still blazing.

Gil But behind us it's pitch black. (*Beat.*) No one around. (*Beat.*) No one anywhere. (*Long pause. Then Gil leans over the hammock and kisses Nick on the mouth. Nick allows it, then pulls back.*)

Nick No.

Gil What do you mean, "no?"

Nick It's time to put away childish things.

Gil . . . Well, I'm sorry, it's a nice quote and all, but that never felt like a childish thing, to me, that never—

Nick (*Moving away.*) How did you find me here anyway? (*Beat.*)

Gil Ruth Corbin.

Nick Ruth Corbin! I don't think I've ever even spoken to Ruth Corbin.

Gil She heard it from Les O'Hare—they're going out now— he got it from, I think, Jackie de Milne, who works with a guy whose wife is best friends with the cousin of that girl you came here with, what's her name—?

Nick Mindy.

Gil Mindy, yes! My research was pretty extensive.

Nick Nothing's going to happen; why did you bother?

Gil Don't you know yet, Nick? I'm here to save you.

Nick (*Bursts out laughing.*) I'm deeply touched.

Gil I have spent months looking for you—I've come to these mountains to get you—who else would climb a mountain for you?

Nick Lili would.

Gil Yes—but when she got there would it matter?

Nick I'm marrying her.

Gil Fine! Wonderful! I have no problems with that—I'm marrying Cinny.

Nick What?

Gil At the end of October; it would please me enormously if you'd agree to be my best man.

Nick You're incredibly perverse.

Gil I'm not perverse, I'm determined to be happy; I'm inventive.

Nick Too inventive.

Gil There can be no such thing. It wasn't even my idea. She kept hinting that she was about to be twenty-four; there was a heavy suggestion that her child-bearing years were drawing to a close. I couldn't let her lie fallow, could I? I think it will be a very good match. She's beautiful, she's smart and she speaks flawless French.

Nick She's rich, too.

Gil Try scoring a point against me with that; see what happens.

Nick I won't try.

Gil I like her a lot—and she's crazy about you.

Nick Is she?

Gil Asks about you constantly. She keeps saying, "Whatever happened to that nice Nick? I think he's my favorite of all your friends."

Nick And what do you say?

Gil I say, "You know what? Mine, too." It's really—it's great.

Nick It's disgusting.

Gil Not at all—I have a plan.

Nick I don't want to know about it.

Gil You have to—it's yours, too—

Nick I already know what mine is.

Gil We marry these women. We become excellent husbands. We prosper. We sire wonderful children. Our families become best friends. And we're . . . us . . . our whole lives. That's my plan.

Nick And no one ever wonders, no one ever suspects?

Gil Who *thinks* that way?

Nick Everyone does.

Gil Nobody does. (*A light goes out somewhere.*)

Nick What was that?

Gil What?

Nick A light went out.

Gil It was from the hotel.

Nick No, it was from the other direction. (*Beat.*)

Gil It was nothing, it was whatever.

Nick That means a light was on. (*Beat.*)

Gil It doesn't matter . . . Jesus, buddy, this paranoia is no good, it just gets in the way, it just gets in the way of what we want.

Nick I don't want the same thing as you. Why don't you just believe that and move on?

Gil I'm sorry, but you lie to the wrong people.

Nick Look—what happened, happened; it's a fact. It's something I did. Maybe it's what you *are*—whatever that means—but for me, it's only a thing I did. It was . . . who knows? . . . It was like kids in boarding school, it was a *phase,* it was just *something that happened* . . . I'm not marrying Lili the way you're marrying Cinny . . .

Gil No—you're having a deep, pure, truthful union.

Nick . . . Okay, *laugh,* but—

Gil I'm not laughing . . . I think that's wonderful. . . . It's what we all want, isn't it? . . . A deep, pure, truthful union? . . . Oh, so, God, so then you've told her about us. (*Pause.*)

Nick No.

Gil You haven't yet? When are you going to? (*Beat.*)

Nick Gil—

Gil Would you like me to? Because I will, you know, if that's what you want, if that's easier for you—(*Pause. Nick starts off.*)

Nick Good night.

Gil No, no, no, you're not going now—

Nick I think that—

Gil Your presence at this moment is not a voluntary thing—

Nick Forget it, I'm—

Gil (*Grabbing his arm roughly.*) Not yet. (*Nick stops.*) Look, when you took off, I said to myself, "Okay, forget this, cut your losses," because that's how I am, but it didn't work. I'd spent too much time on you, it was too big an effort . . . and you say it was, what, a phase? . . . Yeah, well, I was there, too, buddy, and that's not how I remember it. . . . And just because at one sad juncture or another you decided you were a tragic figure, I don't see why my life has to go to pot.

Nick You should lower your voice.

Gil I am whispering in the Catskills. (*Pause.*)

Nick (*With difficulty.*) . . . I couldn't see you . . . I couldn't see anyone . . . I'm sorry if that hurt you . . . I didn't think it would.

Gil I could have helped you, Nicky. I could have been your friend. It's very sad to me that that never occurred to you. . . . It's very sad to me that your whole life was falling apart all the time we were together and you never thought to mention it. I find that *very* sad.

Nick I couldn't—

Gil Why not?

Nick . . . It was a very strange show that was going on . . . and I was trying to . . .

Gil What?

Nick . . . I was trying to dazzle you. (*Pause.*) Oh, look, I've been sort of a mess for a while. I couldn't work. I couldn't think. I've just been running around. . . . Somehow I landed here. I think I may be all right now. Please, please go away. (*Pause.*)

Gil I'm sorry for everything that's ever happened to you. (*Beat.*) So, plan two: We go someplace where we don't have to lie . . . and nobody cares . . . and people give us money for things we do.

Nick When was that planet discovered?

Gil And it never will be . . . but if it were, is that where you'd want to be? (*Nick is silent. Beat.*) Okay, so plan one: We marry these women. And we have our houses and our children . . . and our special friendship. And we have our fine jobs and our fine friends and our fine reputations. And our wives adore us because we're passionate and kind. And our children adore us because we're patient and doting. And we forget about the past—and the world kind of opens wide for us and we laugh like lunatics for the next half-century—because the world thinks it's in love with us . . . the world thinks it's given us everything for free . . . and we know we've stolen the whole damn thing. . . . Isn't that a better idea than your idea?

Nick (*Quietly.*) I think there are some things you don't understand.

Gil I think there's nothing I don't understand. And nothing I'm willing to give up. I think that's the situation. (*Nick has been staring toward the house.*) Why do you keep looking over there?

Nick I'm trying to see Lili.

Gil Why?

Nick . . . Did you hear her before? It didn't matter what Eva said—she didn't care. . . . She's staggering.

Gil Nick—

Nick She's under arrest; there is a moat around her—

Gil Nick, come on—

Nick You don't exist. (*Beat.*)

Gil Goddamn you.

Nick You don't exist. Nothing's ever happened in my life. I'm a man who crosses moats.

Fade Out. End of Scene.

SCENE THREE. *Night. Nick alone. Lili enters.*

Lili Hi.

Nick Hi. (*Beat.*) Are you cold—do you want my jacket?

Lili I'm fine . . .

Nick (*Placing jacket around her shoulders.*) You look . . .

Lili Tell me.

Nick Sleepy.

Lili The doctor brings plenty of pills.

Nick . . . I tried getting to you before, but—

Lili I know; Olivia told me. My mother's asleep now.

Nick She kept heading me off at the pass.

Lili It's one of her best talents; she could teach it. . . . This is the first time I've been outside in days. It's . . . *big* out here, isn't it? (*She laughs.*) I *must* be sleepy. (*Beat.*) Talk.

Nick . . . I'm just . . . looking at you . . .

Lili A drugged young neurotic in a nightdress; it could set sail the fancy of many a man—

Nick That's not what I see.

Lili . . . And that's one of your best talents. (*Beat.*)

Nick I think we have to get you out of here.

Lili Yes.

Nick Do you still want that?

Lili Oh, yes.

Nick And with me?

Lili Why wouldn't I?

Nick ... I've lied to you ... a lot.

Lili Yes, you have. (*Laughs a little.*) I'm sorry—I had a pill a while ago.... I'm not my best after.... Oh God! I'm still hearing her voice, isn't that ... (*Lets the thought trail off.*) ... Nick ... when you build your whole city ...

Nick What?

Lili Make sure there's a roof and a high fence. And don't give away too many keys. (*Beat.*)

Nick Has she been talking about me?

Lili ... She says things ...

Nick I want to explain—

Lili Oh, don't.

Nick You have to let me ... give my version ...

Lili I've heard so many versions; I'm sick of them.... It never happened, okay? Nothing. Just forget it.

Nick I don't think that's possible.

Lili Look.... It doesn't matter that things have happened to you. And I don't care about anything you've ever done. I think you *do* love me. I don't care what it started out to be, we don't ever have to talk about it. Just as long as you're mine now. (*Pause.*)

Nick Lili?

Lili What? (*Pause.*)

Nick Nothing.

Lili What?

Nick Nothing. (*Beat.*)

Lili ... I'm so tired ... I want to sleep with you holding me. If I have to sleep, I want you to hold me.

Nick But if your mother—

Lili Just for a little while.

Nick (*Sitting with her.*) All right.

Lili ... Sing me something!

Nick I don't sing.

Lili Yes—a lullaby.

Nick I don't know any lul—(*Beat.*) Wait ... there was one once, it went.... How did it go? (*Starts to sing in a thin, clear voice.*) "Hush you 'bye/Don't you cry/Go to sleepy little baby ..."

Lili I've never heard this ...

Nick "When you wake/You shall have/All the pretty little horses ..." (*On the brink of sleep, Lili laughs.*)

Fade Out. End of Scene.

SCENE FOUR. *Gil and Eva are seated. Lili and Olivia are looking out towards the lake.*

Eva But you can't go! We'll miss you terribly.

Gil Well, I'll miss all of you, too. You've been awfully nice to me.

Eva What takes you away so suddenly?

Gil It isn't all that sudden. I never intended to stay long.

Eva Has something not worked out for you?

Gil No, I can't say that—I just have trouble staying at leisure too long.

Lili I want to swim!

Eva Out of the question!

Lili I already have my suit on under these clothes. It's not too cold—

Eva You cannot go in alone.

Olivia I'll watch her—

Eva That is not good enough; she is a brand new swimmer—

Lili I'll stay in the shallow part.

Olivia I promise you—nothing will happen to her.

Eva . . . I am outnumbered.

Lili Good!

Gil Well, I guess I'll say goodbye to you now—in case I'm gone when you get out—

Lili Goodbye.

Gil I hope we see each other again some time.

Lili I hope so, too.

Gil Goodbye, Olivia.

Olivia Goodbye.

Lili Beat you there! (*She runs off.*)

Olivia With my blessing. (*She exits.*)

Eva (*Calling to Olivia.*) Keep your eye on her! (*To Gil.*) I hate to see her swim.

Gil But if she stays in the shallow part—

Eva She never stays in the shallow part. . . . It's always a little further, a little further. I wish she'd never learned. Another of your friend's dubious legacies to us.

Gil He's not my friend.

Eva Isn't he? I thought you knew him before.

Gil I know a lot of people who aren't my friends.

Eva My mistake, then. Good. He was so disappointing. Even that says too much for him—You know, I didn't trust him from the moment I saw him.

Gil Is that so?

Eva Oh, yes. It was clear to me right away that he is the sort who takes what is yours and behaves as if it were his own.

Gil Then why did you let Lili—?

Eva Let Lili! Oh, my dear, what a preposterous idea! One does not "let Lili" do anything. If you were to stand with her on the top of the Empire State Building and say, "Please, Lili —do not step over the parapet," she would be a blot on the sidewalk within moments.

Gil Really?

Eva Oh, yes. Lili is someone who must be singed by a thing to keep from being incinerated by it. There is really no controlling her . . . I did think Nick might have gone by now, though. What is it, do you suppose, what is it that makes him stay and stay when he knows he won't be allowed to see her?

Gil He's a nice boy.

Eva A nice boy?

Gil Yeah—he has this conscience.

Eva So a person with a conscience is someone who behaves despicably at all times and, what, feels bad about it after? Spare me people with consciences! They harm my child.

Gil . . . Well, she looks a lot better today than the first time I met her—

Eva That night was not typical—

154

Gil I shouldn't have brought it up—

Eva The ranting and the crying—

Gil What a nightmare.

Eva Awful. Finally she calmed down and fell asleep, but I couldn't sleep. After a while, I went outdoors to get some air. I stared out in space to try to calm myself—and do you know what I saw? Down by the lake where nobody but us ever goes?

Gil . . . What?

Eva Lovers kissing. (*Pause.*)

Gil Huh!

Eva Can you imagine that?

Gil Well . . .

Eva At first, I found it curiously . . . revolting. But, after a while, you know . . . what haven't I seen?

Gil . . . I'd guess . . . not too much. (*Beat.*) Well—

Eva Gil—

Gil Yes?

Eva I was wondering if perhaps you had seen these lovers also.

Gil . . . I think I may have; I think I may have passed them while I took a walk.

Eva . . . Did they seem to you deeply in love? Did it seem to you a thing that would endure?

Gil . . . No. I'd have to say it looked to me like the end of something.

Eva Really?

Gil A pretty bitter one, too.

Eva Well, then it must have been true love!

Gil Who knows?

Eva And true love can always be re-kindled, can't it? If necessary? (*Pause. Gil just looks at her, amazed by her audacity, then considering.*)

Gil . . . Possibly.

Eva That's so interesting—But enough about them, let's get back to you. Now, why did you say you were leaving? Can't we persuade you to stay?

Gil I'd really like to, but . . .

Eva But . . . ?

Gil What would it get me? (*Beat.*) Of course, I could always *revise* what I wanted.

Eva What do you mean?

Gil Well, you know, an alternative incentive could come along. . . . It's like economics—you seek out the situation that brings you the greatest yield.

Eva Do you?

Gil Oh, yeah. It's what economists call "rational."

Eva (*Taking his hand between hers warmly.*) Bless their hearts.

Gil Isn't this a gorgeous day? I think I might stay after all.

Eva Really?

Gil I just wonder if I'll be able to get my old room back at the hotel . . .

Eva Don't worry. I'll have Olivia call.

Gil That's very nice; thank you.

Eva We'll take care of you. (*Looks toward Lili swimming.*) Oh, look how she thrashes! How hard every stroke is for her. My heart dies when I see her . . .

Gil She's your only child, isn't she?

Eva Yes. My only child.

Gil . . . I'm sorry.

Eva Why?

Gil Just that things haven't turned out the way you wished.

Eva Oh my dear, you wish for so many things . . . isn't that so? And you really don't get any of them, do you? . . . Because the world has a wish of its own for you . . . and it's never good. . . . You try to shelter those you love from this wish, you become something you never dreamed. But no. . . . All you may do, really, is stand by, in a kind of horror, until the world has finished and you can collect whatever remains.

Gil . . . It must be awful to believe that. (*Beat. She turns to him.*)

Eva . . . Gil. . . . You revise and revise and revise the thing you want . . . and what are you left with?

Gil Other things you want. The trick is wanting a lot of things. (*He smiles. He starts off.*)

Fade Out. End of Scene.

SCENE FIVE. *Nick and Gil. Night.*

Gil You're shivering.

Nick Yes.

Gil Are you sick?

Nick Yes.

Gil When did you get sick?

Nick I've been getting sick; I've been . . . coming down with something. I can't move. Sometimes I just . . . stay in place.

Gil You're talking to me.

Nick . . . Yes.

Gil That's an improvement. . . . Where does it hurt—here? (*He massages Nick's temples.*)

Nick Yes. There. (*Beat. Gil continues, then moves to his neck.*)

Gil So when are you leaving this place?

Nick We're going tonight.

Gil But you're sick—how can you go when you're sick?

Nick I have to—I've wasted too much time.

Gil Just staring. Just staring across the lake.

Nick Yes.

Gil I've been staring at you staring across the lake. (*Beat. Gil takes his hands off Nick. Nick grabs them and replaces them on his neck. Gil starts off again.*)

Nick I think you hate me.

Gil Why would I hate you?

Nick Because I think. . . . Because I guess you would be right to.

Gil Does it feel like I hate you?

Nick How can I tell?

Gil I'm not strangling you. (*Beat.*)

Nick I think, I think the problem is . . . we never said goodbye, we never really got a chance to say goodbye, I cheated you out of that, I think that's, I think that's the problem.

Gil Could be.

Nick . . . What if . . . we did?

Gil Did what?

Nick Said goodbye . . . what if we said goodbye . . . would you . . . would you go away then, would you leave me alone, then? (*Beat.*)

Gil So how do we do that, say goodbye? How do we arrange it, when? (*Pause.*)

Nick Now. (*Pause.*)

Gil . . . Where else does it hurt? (*Slips his hand inside Nick's shirt.*) Here? (*Nick takes Gil's arm, draws him down; kisses his neck.*)

Fade Out. End of Scene.

SCENE SIX. *Night.*

Lili kneels, staring out. Eva enters behind her.

Eva It's time to go in my darling. He won't be coming for you tonight.

Lili Did Olivia tell you I was here? (*Silence.*) Of course she did . . .

Eva Oh, my darling, my darling . . . The spell is broken—the enchantment is over.

Lili I want to leave here. I want to go tomorrow.

Eva Of course, my darling. First thing in the morning. I'll have Olivia pack the bags and then we'll—

Lili Not home! . . . Anyplace . . . anyplace else. . . . But I won't go home with you . . . (*Still kneeling, she reaches her arms out to her mother who embraces her.*) Not home . . . not home.

Eva . . . But you are my home, *mein kind*. (*The lullaby, "Nicht ist das gluch . . ." plays.*)

Lights Fade. End of Scene.

In the darkness another music takes over—driving late Sixties rock into . . .

SCENE SEVEN. *Ten years later.*

The den of Eva's apartment. Dark with two heavy chairs, a tea table. Windows imagined in the fourth wall. Nick stands looking out a window, downstage. Olivia is there with him.

Nick . . . I guess it's quite a task, dealing with tradesmen.

Olivia Well, you know *her*—first you have to inspect the *goods*—Say it's ham—is it Boar's Head ham or Virginia ham or plain boiled ham? And how much does each kind cost and how much is there of it and is there tax on that? Then how much does she tip or has the boy been rude or what other complaints does she have with the world.

Nick Does this happen all the time?

Olivia We have a lot of delivery people. I can't get her to go out much. Are they still making noise on that street?

Nick It's getting closer.

Olivia Closer? Wasn't it right out the window a few minutes ago?

Nick No, that was at least five blocks away.

Olivia What lungs they have!

Nick I suppose they're . . .

Olivia What?

Nick . . . fueled by righteous indignation.

Olivia Well, who ever wasn't?

Nick . . . Yes. You look exactly the same.

Olivia I've become a very old woman.

Nick Never.

Olivia If that's how you want it, I won't say no. . . . Have you been well? (*Beat.*)

Nick Yes.

Olivia What brings you to New York?

Nick I don't know. . . . Compulsion.

Olivia What?

Nick Accident.

Olivia Yes?

Nick Vacation.

Olivia Oh! Maybe I'll have one of those one of these days.

Nick When I heard the news—

Olivia How did you hear it?

Nick I'm on a lot of grapevines. . . . That's a lie; I've been keeping up . . .

Olivia Oh.

Nick When I heard, I thought, "God, now it's just the two of them."

Olivia Two old maids playing Jewish card games—you don't have to worry about us. Life . . .

Nick . . . Yes?

Olivia I don't have anything to say on the subject. (*Beat.*) I'll get the tea, now. (*She exits. Nick looks out the window again. A long moment, then Lili enters. She is much more grandly dressed than we've ever seen her before—but somehow more severely, as well. She seems older and more studied, harder and more appraising than she used to be.*)

Lili What do you see out my window?

Nick Oh! . . . God, I didn't hear you—

Lili What's going on?

Nick There's a guy with a bullhorn, and a lot of people with signs, and some construction workers, I guess, and I think some Canadian mounties or something . . .

Lili The usual crew.

Nick You see this sort of thing a lot?

Lili It goes on a lot. Mostly, I draw the shades.

Nick We don't get this much out where I am.

Lili I don't suppose you do—Where is that again?

Nick Twenty miles outside of Cincinnati—

Lili My God! And what are you doing?

Nick I'm teaching math at the Dunn-Bradford School.

Lili I've never heard of it. . . . Do you know math?

Nick A little. Enough.

Lili Huh!

Nick . . . I was sorry to hear about your mother.

Lili (*A little distantly.*) Yes . . . we're both orphans now.

Nick (*Taken aback.*) . . . Yes.

Lili Olivia's getting us tea, why don't we sit? You don't hear the noise so much when you're sitting. (*They do.*)

Nick Does it bother you, all of them out there?

Lili Yes.

Nick Just the other day, I was waylaid by a group.

Lili Were you?

Nick Around Columbia. This big hippie parade. God, it was amazing! This . . . smelly, screaming mob! Things flying out of their hair, babies in papooses, flowers everywhere, everybody linking arms; some of them were ripping their clothes off, it was . . . unbelievable, wonderful. I thought, a few years ago I wouldn't even have been able to hallucinate this! (*Lili is staring at him.*) I'm sorry if I'm going on . . . I. . . . Why are you looking at me?

Lili I suppose you never built a whole city.

Nick . . . What? . . . What do you mean?

Lili Once you said that's what you wanted to do. Do you remember? You were asked, what do you want to build? And you said, a whole city. But I guess you never did.

Nick No. I never built anything. (*Beat.*) This room looks exactly the way I always pictured it. Exactly the way you described it to me the first time we met. "Heavy with dark damask," you said.

Lili Did I?

Nick Yes. I remember it exactly. I remember a lot of things exactly, I. . . . Well. I guess now that the place is yours, you'll put new furniture in, won't you? Do it up the way you want it to look.

163

Lili But this is new furniture.

Nick . . . What?

Lili Every piece. I did it all over myself last year. Don't you like it?

Nick . . . Oh. Yes. Of course. I just didn't . . .

Lili What?

Nick I just didn't think this was your taste, that's all.

Lili (*Looks around; as if genuinely wondering.*) Isn't it? (*Beat.*)

Nick Lili . . .

Lili I wonder what's taking Olivia so long. I'd say she was slowing down, but she's always been slow.

Nick I'm sorry. (*Beat.*)

Lili For what?

Nick For what I did to you.

Lili But what an egomaniac you are! Do you really think something you did ten years ago could possibly be of the least consequence?

Nick . . . It's been . . . of consequence to me. (*Lili rises, goes to window.*) Lili—I didn't just run out. It wasn't something I did lightly. I meant to talk to you . . . I always intended to tell you why.

Lili Then why didn't you?

Nick Too much time passed and I didn't know what to say. I wasn't lying to you when I told you I loved you.

Lili This really couldn't matter in the least—

Nick . . . Somebody I'd been in love with came back to

me. . . . There are some people you can't get rid of. This was one.

Lili (*Quietly.*) . . . And did you end up together?

Nick Only for a little while.

Lili Why?

Nick (*Quietly.*) Things didn't work out the way we'd planned.

Lili Oh. (*Beat.*) But you haven't told me who it was. Please tell me. I'd like to know, it will make it feel finished . . . (*Long pause.*)

Nick Her name was Cinny. (*Beat.*)

Lili Cinny?

Nick Yes. She was a girl I knew back home. (*Beat.*) Well, I'm . . . I . . .

Lili Don't feel awkward, it's fine. You're a guest in my home, I'd hate for you to be uncomfortable in any way. We've settled our accounts, now we can be friends.

Nick I'd like that. (*Olivia enters with tea tray.*) Let me help you with that.

Olivia No, that's fine—I'm just setting it down.

Lili Are you going to join us, Olivia?

Olivia I might in just a minute—I want to get my knitting first.

Lili Go do that—we'll help ourselves.

Olivia All right, I will. (*She exits. Lili wanders over to the window.*)

Nick What's happening now?

Lili It's still going on—this one will make the papers, for sure.

Nick It makes me feel about a thousand years old.

Lili (*Her veneer dropping suddenly; during the next beat, it's as if the decade hasn't happened—she's as vulnerable and passionate as she used to be.*) Cinny! My God!

Nick ... What?

Lili Do you really think I didn't know? My mother found out—I didn't care! I wanted you anyway—I would have gone with you anyway—Anything to get out of this place! Anything to get out of this *place*! *I* would have let you have your life—I would have let you have your story, too. You could have built a whole city and I would have lived in it!

Nick Lili...

Lili (*She thrusts out her hand to quiet him. A moment. She composes herself, draws herself up. The ten years have returned. She's almost regal, perfectly philosophical.*) But that is *nicht ahin, nicht ahier*... I haven't poured you any tea. How rude!

Nick ... I'll go.

Lili You have to stay. You have to stay for tea. Do you take sugar? Oh no, I remember, now. No sugar. (*She pours.*) How is it teaching math? Do you enjoy it?

Nick It's ... all right.

Lili I'm glad; it's such a relief to find your place in life, don't you think? (*She hands him tea; he takes it and looks at her.*) You look tired. Maybe I'll sing you a lullaby. You sang me one, once ... remember? I thought it was hilarious!

Nick (*Remembering.*) Then you sang one back to me ...

Lili No. Did I?

Nick Yes. It was something your mother used to sing to you ... some German song ... "Nicht ist ..." "Nicht ist ..."

Lili (*Singing sweetly.*) Nicht ist das gluck fur mich/Es ist fur andre menchen ...

Nick You told me what the words meant ... something like, "There's no such thing as happiness—"

Lili No, wrong again!

Nick What, then? (*Lili drifts toward the window, finds herself looking out it, almost against her will.*)

Lili Happiness exists ...

Nick Happiness exists ...

Lili ... But it's for other people.

Nick That's right ... that's right. (*She stares out the window; he also look straight out.*)

Fade Out. End of Play.

The Author's Voice

For Patti, Kevin, David, and Evan

The Author's Voice

THE AUTHOR'S VOICE was presented as part of Marathon '87 at the Ensemble Studio Theater (Curt Dempster, Artistic Director; Erik Murkoff, Managing Director) in New York City on May 13, 1987. It was directed by Evan Yionoulis; the stage manager was Judith Ann Chew; and the assistant director was Christopher Ashley. The producers of the marathon were John McCormack and Jamie Mendlovitz; the scenic design was by Lewis Folden; the lighting design was by Greg MacPherson; the costume design was by Deborah Shaw; the sound design was by Bruce Ellman; the production stage manager was Nicholas Dunn; associate scenic design was by Elizabeth Kellehere; and the original music was by Ray Leslee. The cast, in order of appearance, was as follows:

Portia Patricia Clarkson

Todd Kevin Bacon

Gene David Pierce

Scene One

*Todd's apartment. Strangely shadowed. A door in the back
wall. A bed obliquely angled into the room. Two chairs and
a table—both dark wood.*

*Lights up on Todd and Portia. They are both young and
beautiful and dressy.*

Portia The author's lair . . .

Todd All right, you've seen it, let's go.

Portia You're joking.

Todd I—

Portia You're serious?

Todd Well—

Portia What? What are you?

Todd Portia.

Portia I'm looking for clues.

Todd . . . Hm.

Portia Tips.

Todd Yes.

Portia Leads.

Todd None here.

Portia It's not . . . exactly . . .

Todd No—

Portia *forthcoming . . .*

Todd Forthcoming?

Portia This room.

Todd (*Sighs with relief.*) No.

Portia You're strange, Todd.

Todd I'm not, not at all.

Portia What's behind that door?

Todd Another apartment. Neighbors.

Portia Really?

Todd Railroad flat. Tenement.

Portia Curious smell.

Todd The neighbors.

Portia Food becomes flesh, somehow, you know?

Todd (*Stymied.*) Of course.

Portia Well, you know those people who trap cooking odors? In their hair—in their down vests—in their—all over, all over themselves?

Todd They're sloppy people, the neighbors.

Portia Do you know them?

Todd We've never met.

Portia They *must* be sloppy people.

Todd Yes. (*He looks puzzled.*)

Portia This isn't what I expected, I must say.

Todd What did you—?

Portia Something cleaner, more pared down, geometric, somehow, I don't know, I can't say. But not this . . . I don't know . . . House of Usher. Do you like living here?

Todd (*Curiously mechanical.*) Sometimes the walls feel like predators, they roam and idle, grow mouths and tongues, close in and bare their teeth; this is what loneliness is to me— living beasts.

Portia (*Beat.*) I've noticed you quote from yourself an awful lot.

Todd What?

Portia That, just now, that was a quotation, wasn't it?

Todd . . . Yes.

Portia From this book of ours, wasn't it?

Todd . . . Yes.

Portia Well, of course I'd realize that, wouldn't I?

Todd . . . Yes. Look, why don't you just go home now, I need—

Portia I've also noticed that, in general, when you're not quoting from yourself, your conversation tends toward the . . .

Todd . . . Toward the . . . ?

Portia Bland.

Todd Ah, the bland, yes.

Portia You're not one of our *glib* authors.

Todd Perhaps . . . (*Searches for the word.*) *not.*

Portia You're beautiful, though.

Todd So are you.

Portia And you write like an angel. How do you write so beautifully?

Todd My writing—

Portia Yes?

Todd It . . . burns in the smithy of my . . . in my smithy.

Portia The torment, I love it. Beauty and pain, what a parlay! Tell me the truth—those aren't the neighbors behind that door. Behind that door, there's some horribly twisted gnome who does all your writing for you—

Todd You had too much to drink tonight . . .

Portia I'm celebrating!

Todd Celebrating what?

Portia Us . . . this teaming, this partnership. Success is absolutely assured; Todd, no, I want you to know that. Those pages you've shown us . . . God, they're incredible. And the jacket photograph *alone* will be a classic. No, I'm sincere. I think you have something important to contribute to literature.

Todd Thank you.

Portia Why are you so nervous?

Todd I'm embarrassed by the smell.

Portia . . . I don't mind.

Todd It embarrasses me.

Portia I think it's sexy.

Todd It's not.

Portia It is—

Todd No—

Portia I swear—

Todd Tonight it's not.

Portia (*Beat.*) You want me to go.

Todd You've noticed.

Portia You're the fevered type.

Todd A little.

Portia And tomorrow you must rise early and have your jog and your protein shake and then spill your pain at the type-writer. Hours and hours wiggling the loosened tooth of your despair.

Todd I guess.

Portia I'm sorry I've invaded your territory. I needed to see, though. I'm not one of those casual editors. I can't just tighten your syntax. I need to *see*, to *know*, to *absorb*, to *live through*, to *live with*, to *contemplate*, to *understand*. To *understand*. (*She kisses him passionately*.) Good night. (*She exits. Todd sits at the table for a long moment. The door in the back creaks open. A horribly twisted gnome emerges, carrying a sheaf of papers. He goes to Todd and hands him the pages. Todd accepts them. They look at each other. Fadeout*.)

Scene Two

Todd reading. The gnome, Gene, watches.

Gene You *balked.*

Todd This is wonderful. Is it?

Gene The moment came—the decisive moment—and you let it slip by. That's unforgivable.

Todd The pain, the sheer . . . *pain;* it's painful, right?

Gene Was it because of me?

Todd I'll send this off first thing tomorrow. Portia will think she inspired me. Will she like it?

Gene What?

Todd The chapter.

Gene Yes. She will.

Todd You're sure?

Gene I'm sure . . .

Todd Because I can't tell—

Gene I'm sure—

Todd Because I don't seem to have a feel for—

Gene I'M SURE!

Todd Touchy, touchy, touchy.

Gene She was beautiful, wasn't she?

Todd Who?

Gene The girl.

Todd Which . . . ?

Gene Tonight.

Todd Portia.

Gene Yes.

Todd (*Thinks a moment.*) Yes. I think so. Yes.

Gene You *think* so?

Todd I wasn't paying close attention. That sort of thing gets stale. (*Gene lets out a strangled howl.*)

Gene You *appall* me.

Todd She was beautiful.

Gene I saw.

Todd *What?*

Gene There's a keyhole, you know. A slit at the bottom of the door. Slants of light. This room made visible. I moved, I watched, I saw—

Todd Son-of-a-bitch—

Gene Not the whole picture, but . . . hair and . . .

Todd Son-of-a-bitch—

Gene —calves and ankles and once, I think—

Todd I told you—

Gene —an elbow—

Todd I told you not to move when she was here. I told you to act like a churchmouse.

Gene I *am* a churchmouse—

Todd She was curious enough without hearing sounds—

Gene She was curious, you—

179

Todd Don't you know how fragile this whole deal is—

Gene You nipped that curiosity in the bud, I noticed—the *neighbors*!

Todd She can't find out about this, Gene, or it's over, all over, we're through.

Gene Is that a *bad* thing?

Todd Not again, please. Not again. That damned . . . what is it called, something you say over and over?

Gene Litany.

Todd That damned litany, over and over! Yes, it would be a bad thing. What we have, this is a good thing. If it ended, it would be a bad thing.

Gene Not for me.

Todd Oh, please . . .

Gene Despised, sequestered, denied even the standard compensations, I would relish the termination of all—

Todd Do you want me to put you back where I found you? (*Beat.*)

Gene (*Quietly.*) No.

Todd In the gutter.

Gene In the gutter! What a cliché. I was in an alley.

Todd Starving and crying—

Gene And carrying pages of precious material which you promptly sold to the highest—

Todd I took you in!

Gene You took me for everything I had; it was not Nightingale in the Crimea.

Todd I brought the pages to a party—could you have done that? I met Portia there—could you have done that? She said, "This is a work of . . . this is a work of . . ."

Gene Genius—

Todd Genius! Yes! I let her take me to lunch, I worked my charm, I finessed her into a contract—

Gene Thus began my stellar career!

Todd And it's good! (*Gene stares at him fiercely, then lets out a beastly roar. Beat.*) That sort of thing has got to stop.

Gene Why did you let her go tonight?

Todd I wasn't interested.

Gene How can you not be interested?

Todd These things repeat themselves.

Gene *They*—!

Todd —get dull—

Gene *I*—

Todd My libido wavers.

Gene *Use mine!*

Todd I'm going to bed.

Gene You never bring anyone home! Some nights you don't come home yourself! I wait. I sit. I don't move. It hurts to move anyway. My body is sore. My muscles ache from disuse and misshapenness. I sit in that patch of darkness, that cupboard that has been allotted me, and stare out at an airshaft and wait for some noise from the hallway, some stirring, for *you* . . . and you don't come. Why don't you bring one home? I'd be still as a churchmouse. I'd hold my breath. I want to hear it, to peek through the keyhole and see it. Live. Unrehearsed. The whole event. I would be so grateful.

Todd Please stop talking and go to sleep before I say something true that will hurt you.

Gene I *wash*. Hour after hour, I scrub, I pummice! I'm meticulously clean. The smell comes from *airlessness*. From being alone with myself in a dark room. It's the smell of *imprisonment,* let me out and it will go away!

Todd You can't go out!

Gene You don't let me.

Todd Don't dare.

Gene Just for a stroll. A walk on the street. I need books! If I'm to live in a purely verbal universe, I must have my vocabulary replenished every now and then. Let me buy books and I'll come right back and be happy—

Todd I get you whatever books you need, you know that—

Gene I need to see people walking on the street—

Todd No fits tonight, I'm too tired.

Gene My needs are not being attended to!

Todd You don't want to go out, you know you don't, you know it—

Gene Just for an afternoon—

Todd They *laugh* at you on the street.

Gene *Not always.*

Todd *Mostly they do!* (*Beat.*)

Gene (*Softly.*) Mostly they do. (*He goes quietly to his room, closes the door. Todd lies down on the bed. A knocking starts* *from behind the door. Pauses. Starts again. Pauses. From behind the closed door.)* Todd—?

Todd Yes—?

Gene What's in it for you? (*Todd puts pillow over his head and turns over. Fadeout.*)

Scene Three

A flash goes off in the dark. Lights up. Portia is taking Polaroids of Todd.

Portia Now, don't get offended!

Todd I'm not offended.

Portia The higher-ups simply think—and in a way I agree with them—they simply think—here, hold this. (*She hands him photo.*) They simply think the book, as it stands, is a little *spineless*, that's all—Pose. (*He poses.*)

Todd Spineless?

Portia Lacking a spine.

Todd Ah!

Portia The quality of the—of the what?—of the *feeling*, of the emotional, you know, *milieu*—is immaculately rendered, but there seems to be no, no thrust, no action, no event. Right now it's sort of lumpy, sort of pudding-y, a kind of *mousse* of despair, if you know what I—Not that that's *bad*—we're all agreed despair is due for a revival. Here, hold this. (*She hands him photo.*) We're simply suggesting you incorporate more of the, you know, you make it less *endoscopic,* if you know what I—Pose. (*He poses.*)

Todd I don't know how to do that.

Portia Oh, Todd, oh, Todd . . .

Todd What does that mean, oh, Todd, oh, Todd?

Portia I know your nightlife.

Todd That's irrelevant.

Portia It's superficial; it's not irrelevant.

Todd I could never possibly . . . write . . . I could never possibly write that.

Portia Hold this. (*She hands him photo.*)

Todd These are grotesque.

Portia They're just jacket ideas, they're not the real thing.

Todd Do I look like this?

Portia Of course not.

Todd How do I look?

Portia Like Todd.

Todd I mean, how do I look to *you*? (*Portia sits on him.*)

Portia Nice.

Todd Portia—

Portia Todd.

Todd Please get off me.

Portia Aren't you attracted to me?

Todd I don't remember.

Portia What?

Todd I sometimes empty out.

Portia What?

Todd I can't muster enthusiasm. I forget. My body remembers but I forget.

Portia Is that, what, is that some sort of Zen *koan* or something, what is that?

Todd Please.

Portia What is it with you, Todd?

Todd Portia—

Portia Don't hide from me, Todd. There's no need. Don't you know? There is nothing about you too dark, too hideous, no single thing too ugly for me to accept, embrace, and love. (*She moves to kiss him.*)

Todd I need to do re-writes.

Portia It's come over you?

Todd What—?

Portia Inspiration?

Todd Yes!

Portia I'll go. (*Dismounts him.*) Now, remember: a story, a spine, facts! Bring in your club days, bring in your sex life! Make me a book I can sell!

Todd Yes.

Portia Wait a second.

Todd What?

Portia Have the neighbors moved?

Todd . . . Why?

Portia The smell is gone. (*She kisses two fingers, waves with them, and exits.*)

Todd . . . Gene? (*He approaches Gene's room.*) Gene! (*He opens the door, bangs violently around the room.*) GENE! (*Blackout.*)

Scene Four

Todd is seated at the table. Gene wears a long coat, dark glasses, a fedora. By his side, there is a package of books.

Gene It came to me: Why not? (*Beat.*) You were gone and I wasn't physically restrained. The outside world might be a painful place but every place is a painful one, so why not? (*Beat.*) I put on your greatcoat and your glasses and your fedora and looked hardly abnormal at all. I was careful, Todd, don't look at me like that, I was so careful, no neighbor saw, not the super, no one, I walked in shadows *exclusively.* (*He smiles hopefully.*) I know you've taken me on at great financial and personal sacrifice to yourself, I know I've altered your life completely, I know with me on your hands no sane life is possible, I'm grateful, I truly am, I'm not an ingrate, *don't look at me like that!* (*Beat. He picks up the books.*) I got these at a used-book store, a place, I swear to you, as musty as myself. I fit right in. (*Beat.*) Todd, I had to do this for both of us. I was forgetting things; words lost their attachments. Without this little trip, this one, one-time-only little trip, you would have had a book full of nonsense, a mere *crunch* of syllables. (*Beat.*) It's not a place I want to go to anymore, the world. I promise. (*Beat.*) *This isn't fair!* (*Beat.*) Look: burn this coat, buy another on our royalties! Another hat, too, and new glasses, I know I'm an infection, I won't be insulted! Please, please talk! I'm sure I must have been laughed at on the street, you don't have to worry . . . (*Beat.*) Please . . . (*Beat.*)

Todd (*Quietly.*) Come here . . .

Gene Why?

Todd Come here . . .

Gene Why?

Todd I want to hold you. (*Pause.*)

Gene . . . Todd?

Todd Please. (*Gene approaches gingerly as Todd stretches out his arms. Gene is about to enter them when Todd grabs his wrist and wrestles him to the ground, getting him in a hammerlock. Gene howls, tries to twist his way out of the lock, rolls. Todd rolls with him, gets him into the lock again.*) SON-OF-A-BITCH! (*Gene cries out in blinding pain.*) NEVER DO THAT AGAIN! (*Gene cries out.*) DO YOU HEAR ME? (*Gene cries out again.*) DO YOU HEAR ME! (*Gene utters a strangled, rattling cry, manages to dodge out of Todd's grip and crawl a few inches away. Todd leaps on top of him, lies flat on him, crushing him into the ground.*) Do you hear me?

Gene Y-E-E-E-E-S!!!!!!!!!!!!!! (*Todd springs off him, falls panting onto the bed. Gene crawls to his room, as quickly as he can from fear, but still haltingly, jerkily. He kicks the door shut. A long moment.*)

Todd Gene . . . ? (*Beat.*) Gene . . . ? (*Beat.*) Gene . . . ?

Gene We're over. (*Fadeout.*)

Scene Five

Todd stands at the door, a liquor bottle in his hand. From Gene's room, an incessant keening, a mournful animal sound. Todd knocks his palm against the door. Again. Again. Again. Again.

Todd Christ, I'm sorry! (*Beat.*) I didn't mean to hurt you. Please come out. (*Beat.*) Please come out. (*Beat.*) I'm not a cruel person. I'm not . . . (*Beat. The keening subsides.*) Gene? (*Beat.*) Gene, are you all right, now? (*Beat. Still quiet.*) Are you better? You sound better. (*Still quiet.*) (*Beat.*) Gene, listen, I'm going to do like we used to, okay? Remember? I'm going to tell you something that happened to me and you can tell me what it means, remember? Okay? (*Beat.*) Is that okay? (*Beat.*) Okay. (*He sits with his back against the door.*) This happened the other day at the health club. You know, where I go? (*Beat.*) Right. Well, I was going to take a swim. I'd never used the pool there before but I wanted to swim. So I was getting suited up when a man at the row of lockers across from me started talking to his friend. This man, he was balding, but he seemed pretty fit, and he was pleased with himself, you could tell, like he didn't even mind being bald, and I thought, well, if I feel like that at his age, I won't be doing half-bad. And his friend looked pretty good, too, and it sort of cheered me up. Anyway, they went to the pool. I finished getting ready, and then I went to the pool. It was just the three of us and an attendant. The attendant yelled at me, "No trunks!" I didn't understand. Then I looked at the two men swimming in the pool. They were naked. It was policy. When they were naked like that, they didn't look so good. They looked fat. They looked like fish—large . . . extinct . . . fish . . . I bent to take off my trunks. As I did, the bald man came up for air. For a second, he was completely still, frozen

189

solid in the water. He looked at me and kept looking. I dove in, a perfect dive with a flip and a spin. When I came up for air, the bald man wasn't in the pool anymore. He was standing by the poolside, crying hysterically. His friend was next to him, trying to calm him down, but the bald-headed man wouldn't stop crying. "Why are you crying?" his friend kept asking. "It was the dive," he said. "It was the dive." (*Beat.*) Gene . . . ? (*Beat.*) Gene, why did that make him cry? (*Beat.*) Why?. . . Why did that make him cry? (*Beat.*) Gene . . . ? Gene . . . ? Why?

Gene (*From the bedroom; braying.*) BECAUSE IT WAS *SAD*! (*Beat.*)

Todd Oh. (*Beat.*) I need you to tell me these sorts of things, Gene. I can't figure them out on my own. (*Beat.*) My life isn't good. You think it is, but it's not. Once is was, but it's not anymore. (*Beat.*) I used to be made happy by . . . stupid things. Looking in the mirror! I looked so hard I didn't recognize myself. I got scared, Gene! I didn't know where I was half the time. Then, I found you. (*Beat.*) Make me famous, Gene. I want to be famous. People will photograph me and write about me. I'll study how they see me and live inside it . . . It'll be like a home. (*Pause.*) I'll give you what you want. I won't deny you anymore. Anything I can, I'll give you. (*Beat. Gene emerges from the room. He embraces Todd. Todd moans. Fadeout.*)

Scene Six

Todd and Gene. Todd dressing for the evening.

Gene The scene must be played beautifully.

Todd I don't know if I can do this.

Gene You don't have a choice. I'll stop writing if you don't. I'll go back to the streets, find another benefactor. Or die, I don't care which.

Todd All right. But what do I say? It's been a long time . . .

Gene I'll write the scene for you. You simply play it out.

Todd (*Sighs.*)

Gene You come up behind Portia . . .

Todd Yes . . .

Gene Fling an arm across her chest—

Todd That's melodramatic—

Gene *You fling an arm across her chest—*

Todd Yes, yes, all right, fine—

Gene And you say, "Darling, I want you." (*Beat.*)

Todd I say, what?

Gene "Darling, I want you."

Todd I don't say that.

Gene You do.

Todd She'd laugh in my face.

Gene Never.

Todd You're insane.

Gene (*Insistently.*) "Darling, I want you."

Todd The only words I could possibly get away with in that whole sentence are "I" and "you."

Gene You will say this! You will say, "Darling, I want you." She will be moved by the poetic simplicity of your expression! (*Beat.*)

Todd Fine.

Gene Then—you will turn her toward you, kiss each shoulder, her neck, then rise ever so slowly till your lips meet hers. You will kiss her, and say, "Be mine." (*Beat. Todd looks at him skeptically.*) Then—

Todd Wait a minute—

Gene What?

Todd That won't work.

Gene It will work like a *dream*—

Todd Trust me on this—

Gene Like a *dream*—

Todd She will be out of here in fourteen seconds flat.

Gene Nonsense.

Todd I promise you.

Gene Nonsense.

Todd I *promise* you. (*Beat.*)

Gene What would you say—what *do* you say, then, in circumstances like these? There's a woman, there's a bed, you're alone, you're enchanted, what do you say? (*Beat.*)

Todd Do you want to sleep with me?

Gene A-A-A-R-G-H!!!!

Todd I'm sorry.

Gene You don't understand.

Todd I do—

Gene You don't understand the situation.

Todd Inform me.

Gene You are *enraptured*. You are . . . *transported*. This is no common *lay*. This is no cheap *one-nighter*. The finest fibers of your being quiver in expectancy. Poetry floods your soul. "Do you want to sleep with me?" simply will not suffice, not this night. What do you say, then? When all the beauty of the universe churns inside you. (*Beat. Todd thinks.*)

Todd Are you staying?

Gene A-A-A-R-G-H!!!!!!

Todd Gene—

Gene A-A-A-R-G-H!!!!!!

Todd Gene—

Gene The world *requires* me—

Todd Gene—

Gene —to rewrite its wretched *dialogue*!

Todd Gene—

Gene You will make it beautiful. You will proceed as I describe. You will *say*, "Darling, I want you." You will say, "Be mine." You will be tender and slow and romantic. You will *make it work!* (*Beat.*)

Todd Not a word from you.

Gene . . . I know.

Todd Not a peep.

Gene I promise.

Todd For your own good as well as mine. You know I act for both of us, don't you? You know I want the best for both of us?

Gene . . . Yes.

Todd I'll be back soon. (*He exits. Gene looks after him, waits until he's sure he's gone. Then he approaches Todd's bed. He touches it carefully.*)

Gene Todd . . .? (*Gene runs his hands across the bed, feeling the smooth, silky textures.*) Todd . . . it wouldn't be bad if she saw me. Not so bad. (*He climbs onto the bed.*) Often beautiful women come upon hideous men and love them. They uncover an inner beauty, oh, and crowns of light weave into canopies over their heads and the carbuncles and the cicatrices, the humps and wens miraculously disappear. The beasts are replaced by angels. She'll see me, Todd, she'll see. And you'll be loved for me. (*Fadeout.*)

Scene Seven

Todd's room in half-light—a golden shaft spilled across the floor. Todd and Portia enter. The picture they make in this light is burnished and lovely. Lights come up slightly fuller.

Portia You were brilliant tonight. You didn't even have to *speak* is how brilliant you were. I loved when we went to that place with the flashing lights and your face came floating up at me in patches, it was poetry, truly poetry. I was speaking to the big boys today, Todd. They want to take you to lunch; they're very excited, really thrilled. Everything's mapped out, your whole itinerary. The book jacket's designed, there are display cases ready, and we're putting your photograph on billboards all over the city. All we need now is a book . . .

Todd I'm working slowly.

Portia No matter. I have faith in you. I believe in you. (*Beat.*) This night has been sensational. You actually invited me in. (*Beat.*) Todd?

Todd (*Grabbing her from behind.*) Darling, I want you . . .

Portia What? (*Beat.*)

Todd Darling, I want you. (*She turns, laughs in his face, and in one elegant but blindingly quick motion, whips her dress off over her head.*) Hey—(*She starts undressing him.*)

Portia This will have to be quick; I have an early day tomorrow.

Todd Wait! I have to kiss you slowly, I have to—

Portia I've been wondering what your problem was—

Todd Portia, I— (*She has his shirt off, is starting on his pants.*)

Portia I was beginning to think you were gay—

Todd Turn around—

Portia You always wonder about that. Could you shrug out of these? (*He shrugs out of his pants. Portia lies on the bed.*) Thank you. Now be careful, I'm getting my period, I'm a little sensitive—

Todd Wait—

Portia I know this is not the best time to start some sort of blazing romance, but you were just so damned *slow*.

Todd (*Kneels on bed, grabs her hand.*) Be mine! (*Beat. She laughs in his face.*)

Portia Christ, Todd, where are you getting these lines? Come on. (*She starts to pull off his underpants; he stops her, moves away from her.*)

Todd Wait!

Portia What?

Todd This is not going well . . .

Portia I think it's going pretty well. I think most people would think it was going pretty well . . .

Todd (*Pulling her off the bed.*) You don't understand.

Portia What?

Todd Turn around . . .

Portia Todd . . .

Todd *Turn around.* (*Beat. She turns around. He puts his arm across her chest.*) Be mine.

Portia Look, do you want to sleep with me?

Todd Portia—

Portia Am I staying?

Todd You're doing everything wrong!

Portia What are you talking about?

Gene (*From his room.*) IT'S SUPPOSED TO BE BEAUTIFUL! (*A deathless pause.*)

Portia Todd . . .

Todd Oh, Jesus . . .

Portia What was that, Todd?

Todd Nothing.

Portia That wasn't nothing. That was a voice, saying—

Gene (*From bedroom.*) IT'S SUPPOSED TO BE BEAUTIFUL!

Portia Jesus Christ, what's the deal here? (*Gene flings open the door.*)

Gene Am I the only one left with a sense of loveliness? (*Portia stares at him in horror.*)

Portia Oh my God . . . oh my God . . .

Todd Gene . . .

Gene (*Coming out of the room.*) Look at the two of you . . . You are . . . trustees of beauty . . . You shine with grace . . . How have you managed to avoid minimal interior fineness?

Portia Todd . . . (*Gene approaches her.*)

Gene Don't you know what you're supposed to do now? Don't you know your part?

Portia Todd . . .

Todd Oh, Jesus . . .

Gene You see me and you are not repelled. You draw in. You come closer and closer. The closer you get, the handsomer I become. You touch me. You kiss me. (*He kisses her.*) I stand tall. (*She faints. Todd catches her.*) No. You don't know your part at all. (*He closes his eyes. Fadeout.*)

Scene Eight

Gene is bent half on a chair, half on the table, hands spread flat before him almost in an attitude of supplication. He is moaning softly, his eyes closed. Todd laces into him.

Todd I *lied*, I *finessed* the situation. I said you were an *intruder*. The crazed, hideous neighbor breaking down the door between us. I *calmed* her down. I said this was an *unprecedented* event. I said I was contacting the authorities *immediately*. I said it would *never* happen again.

Gene O-o-o-o-h-h . . .

Todd And it's not going to, either. There aren't going to be any more little jaunts, Gene. No more charming trips into the street. No more expeditions into the living room. From now on, you lock yourself in that room, and you don't come out until there's a book, a goddamn publishable item! *Do you understand me!*

Gene I can't . . .

Todd What are you talking about?

Gene I can't go on . . .

Todd *What are you talking about!*

Gene . . . She fainted . . .

Todd Oh, Jesus . . .

Gene I lived for the moment I would blossom at a kiss and she fainted!

Todd I don't want to hear this, now!

Gene I can't, I can't possibly go on . . .

Todd *Listen to me!* You *will* go on. You will . . . do what I demand of you. You will find a story and . . . pick the words you need and . . . get a *spine* and *make me a book!* Do you *understand?*

Gene . . . I can't . . .

Todd You will *do it! Do you understand!* (*He slaps him.*) *Do you understand!* (*He slaps him again.*)

Gene (*Roaring it out.*) YES! (*Todd pulls Gene up out of the chair.*)

Todd Then *start!* (*Todd throws Gene toward his room. He lands hunched in the doorway, his back to us. Todd sits, controls himself.*) Gene . . . ?

Gene . . . What?

Todd I didn't mean to be harsh.

Gene . . . Ah.

Todd I just wanted you to know that. (*Gene turns sharply; looks at Todd. Fadeout.*)

Scene Nine

Gene sits at the table, smiling. A small gift-wrapped package is on the table. Todd bursts in, effusive.

Todd I just got word! We're already into a second printing. That's extremely unusual on a publication day.

Gene Ah!

Todd And three reviews came out—all raves!

Gene Lovely.

Todd (*Reading.*) "When a book receives as much hype as *Drift* has, and when, in addition, its author looks more like a model for cologne than like Herman Melville, this critic is naturally inclined to skepticism. That proves unfounded here, however; because *Drift* is a knockout, far and away the best first novel of the season, perhaps the decade." Do you believe it?

Gene Very nice.

Todd I have to thank you.

Gene Oh, no . . .

Todd No, I do. I know things weren't always . . . pleasant . . . between us, but look what it got you to do! Gene, I can say it now. I was amazed how you worked! Once you got started, it took you, what, three weeks? And that from scratch! You ditched all the material you had before and just started. I used to listen, I can tell you this now, I listened at the door to the typewriter clattering away, nonstop, it just *thundered* out of you!

Gene Yes.

Todd When I go on talk shows, Gene—I want you to know this—I'm always asked, "How do you write?" And do you know what I say? I say, "A demon lives with me." I mean, you. I want you to know that. For vanity's sake . . .

Gene You're very kind.

Todd The review starts by quoting the entire opening paragraph! "I live alone. There are no neighbors. There is no neighborhood. Brick has vanished. Tree and sky, too. When I peer through the narrow, grimy shaft that is my window, I see horizon and murk." He says it's the most memorable opening since, "Call me Ishmael."

Gene (*Indicating package.*) This is for you.

Todd What?

Gene For you.

Todd What?

Gene A present.

Todd (*Touched.*) . . . Gene!

Gene Open it.

Todd I don't know what to say . . .

Gene I wanted to give you this for publication day. A memento.

Todd (*Unwraps it.*) A book. *Layaway.* Thank you.

Gene I found it that day I was a bad boy . . . remember? . . . It's very obscure. Canadian. It was out-of-print but it called to me. I used the phone when you were out. I was so moved, I tracked the author down and spoke to him.

Todd Really?

Gene I hope you don't mind.

Todd Of course not. I'm very touched that you'd think of me.

Gene Read some.

Todd Now?

Gene Yes, please. It's one of my favorite books, ever. I think I'm the only one who's ever read it, but it may gain shortly in prestige.

Todd (*Reads.*) "I live alone. There are no neighbors. There is no neighborhood . . ."

Gene That resonates, doesn't it?

Todd (*Reading on in horror.*) "Brick has vanished. Tree and sky, too. When I peer through the narrow, grimy shaft that is my window. . ."

Gene So Canadian . . .

Todd ". . . I see horizon and murk. . . ."

Gene Do you like it?

Todd (*Flipping in horror through the book.*) Every word . . . You stole every word!

Gene The author has such a strong voice, don't you think? Truly distinctive. It comes right out of him. He's sickly, he told me. Stooped and scarred. Unfortunate looks. He should be calling any minute. Be kind to him. (*Todd doubles over, clutches himself, lets out an almost silent cry.*) I hear he's in tremendous pain. (*Gene looks at Todd. Fadeout.*)

End of Play

Hurrah at Last

For David Warren and Peter Frechette

Hurrah at Last was commissioned and originally produced by South Coast Repertory and was produced by Roundabout Theater Company (Todd Haimes, Artistic Director) at the Gramercy Theatre in New York City, on June 3, 1999. It was directed by David Warren; the set design was by Neil Patel; the costume design was by Candice Donnelly; the lighting design was by Peter Maradudin; and the sound design was by John Gromada. The cast was as follows:

Thea Ileen Getz

Laurie Peter Frechette

Eamon Kevin O'Rourke

Oliver Paul Michael Valley

Gia Judith Blazer

Sumner Larry Keith

Reva Dori Brenner

Thunder Dreyfus

How strange the truth appears at last!
I feel as old as worn out shoes:
I know what I have lost or missed,
Or certainly will some day lose
I know the follies whom I kissed,
Whom self-deception will accuse—

And yet this knowledge, like the Jews,
Can make me glad that I exist!
Although I must my self accuse
Not when I win, but when I lose:
Although this knowledge comes and goes,
Although the wind and the rain persist:
How I am glad that I exist!
    With a hey ho, the stupid past,
    And a ho ho, a ha ha and a hurrah at last.

              —Delmore Schwartz

ACT ONE

SCENE 1. (*An enormous, sprawling, expensive loft apartment, Christmas Eve. Laurie sits in his coat. Thea is distributing hors d'oeuvres plates all around the apartment.*)

Laurie Destitute. In a word. No, not me, don't worry, not *me*, but everyone around me. Perfectly ordinary, middle class—*urban* middle class people—who got used to some small sense of privilege—and now find themselves *without funds*—eating *peanut* butter, for crying out—and what can you tell them? I think that's why I have this cold—oh, and then there's Oliver's play—I really think I just can't be in a town that *fetes* Oliver's play—

Thea Oliver loves you—

Laurie And I love Oliver, but his *play* is detritus—and as for his loving me—that's another story—

Thea He's coming—

Laurie Well, yes, that's fine; with Gia?

Thea Of course.

Laurie That will be scintillating—

Thea She's lovely.

Laurie I know she's lovely, My God!—well as much as you *can* know it of someone with whom you share no language, although that doesn't seem to have disturbed Oliver much— oh the bile! The bile! Do you hear it? I've got to get away for a bit.

Thea Didn't you love his new play?

Laurie Whose?

Thea Oliver's. So charming. So gifted.

Laurie Thea, have you listened to nothing I've said?

Thea I can't really hear you in that sector of the apartment.

Laurie Then you let me just natter on—

Thea Oh, yes. Feel free. Why don't you take off your coat?

Laurie I have a cold.

Thea That makes it *worse*—

Laurie You are *such* a mother.
  (*Beat. Thea walks away, wounded.*) Oh, oh—oh—oh—
I'm—sorry—I didn't mean to . . . do *that*.

Thea I'm sure.

Laurie Look, the thing is the other day I was sitting in a bar
with this macho poet who once won a big grant, and he was
literally crying into his bourbon because it's winter and his
coat is threadbare—this brilliant (well, competent) writer—
this guy who hunts!

Thea That's sad.

Laurie I know. It was sort of strapping and Dickensian in one
depressing rush; anyway it made me very jealous of my coat.

Thea Was he asking you for money, this poet?

Laurie How could he? I don't have any! No, no, I mean—I
live from tiny windfall to tiny windfall—and I have the good
fortune to be related to some people who, if I don't say
anything too truthful, will see me through anything that I
might—but I'm closer to *him* than I am to *you*—as far as
money goes—so—no, I'm *fine*. Listen, the thing about Oliver
is, they want him to write the screenplay of my book.

Thea Oh, fabulous! He's *such* an incredible writer.

Laurie Thea.

Thea Don't you just love his new play?

Laurie Yes. I found the second act . . . faintly carcinogenic, but otherwise—

Thea Laurie, we tried again last week.

Laurie What? Oh.

Thea It didn't take.

Laurie Oh, I'm so sorry.

Thea There's no baby. We have to start all over again.

Laurie Oh God, that's so expensive, I mean heartbreaking.

Thea We have to start all over.

Laurie Is it—? Have you ever—No, I won't.

Thea What?

Laurie Considered buying a Chinese one.

Thea No.

Laurie I mean, it isn't your eggs. And Eamon's sperm, well just contains little Eamons, doesn't it, which is *lovely* but . . . you know . . .

Thea Sweetie, I know you have no meanness *in* you. But sometimes I think that's because it's always coming *out* of you.

Laurie I'm just really trying to think of a solution, that's all.

Thea That's not the one for us.

Laurie Why *not?*

Thea (*Crosses to a distant part of the room.*) We at least want it to be part—

Laurie And what is this mania for babies, anyway? I know I speak outside the realm of—philoprogenitivity—and all—but, so what, a baby? I mean, yes, I know, they're awfully charming—for *people*—but that stops—and then you have this—irreversible event—reflecting badly on you—for the rest of time. I don't think I've given a moment of joy to Mom and Dad—

Thea They're coming by the way—

Laurie —and *you* please them only at the expense of your identity: *She married well* is what they love about you. You had authentic perversity once upon a time, and now all you do is dish out these overly complex canapés that you learned to make under the tutelage of this domestic fascist who seems to have colonized the formerly independent minds of your entire generation; and I wonder, aren't you at all inclined to ask yourself, *what's happened?* To review your own history? To re-shape the arc and plan of your life according to some worthier wisdom? *Aren't you?*

Thea (*From a distance.*) I'M SORRY, I CAN'T HEAR YOU.

Laurie I SAID: I DON'T HAVE ANY MONEY!

Thea (*Crossing to him.*) Do you need money?

Eamon (*Enters on phone.*) Do you need money?

Laurie . . . No. I'm fine.

Eamon Any time; just ask.

  (*He exits.*)

Thea He *means* that.

Laurie I know. I exaggerate.

Thea He loves you.

Laurie (*Sighs heavily.*) Everyone does.
  Did you say Mom and Dad are coming?

Thea I invited them.

Laurie What were you *thinking*?

Thea It's Christmas.

Laurie So?

Thea They had nowhere else to go.

Laurie So?

Thea I couldn't stand to think of them alone at Christmas.

Laurie Thea, we're Jews.

Thea Whatever.

Laurie We're not supposed to be toasting the holiday, we're supposed to be at the movies; it's in the Pentateuch.

Thea I love Christmas.

Laurie Well, you're allowed. Your husband is Eamon O'Bryan; you married the Yule log—I just feel deracinated.

Thea I'm sorry to contribute to your alienation.

Laurie Well. Ho hum.
   I'm sorry you're not pregnant.

   (*Eamon enters.*)

Eamon Good news! Abby's coming to the party!

   (*He disappears again.*)

Thea (*Sullen.*) Oh, good.
   (*Thea and Laurie exchange a look, grim. Changing subject.*) But I'm so glad that Oliver's going to be adapting your book.

Laurie Yes.

Thea His new play is really wonderful.

Laurie That's what I hear.

Thea That Oliver. I mean, can you imagine? To be *so* talented and *so* successful and *so* good-looking and so *nice*! Is it coincidence? Did you recommend him?

Laurie I didn't recommend him—

Thea Then what an amazing thing!

Laurie I'd sort of hoped to be—yes, amazing!—I'd sort of hoped to be doing it my—

Thea He understands you so well—

Laurie Well, he pays a lot of at*ten*tion to me, at any—

Thea He adores you, he worships you—

Laurie And there's absolutely *no money* in it—

Thea He's in love with you, in some peculiar way.

Laurie Yes. He is. And it is.

Thea Wait.
  You *do* think he's a good writer, don't you?

Laurie Of course I do. He's a wonderful writer.
  (*Beat.*) No, he is.

Thea Laurie—

Laurie I think he's *terribly* wealthy.

Thea That's terrific, that's great.

Laurie I think he has a lot of money.

Thea Well—

Laurie But I'm not certain—I mean, he won't *tell* me—how much—

Thea Do you ask?

Laurie Not exactly, not literally, but any sensitive person could tell that's where I'm heading—

Thea That's so vulgar—

Laurie —but he *refuses* to tell me. I think he would show me his penis if I asked. No I'm certain of it. I could say, "Oliver, show me your penis," and his pants would be on the floor. But a simple accounting of his finances is beyond—

Thea Well, I don't—

Laurie How much money do *you* have?

Thea I'm not going to tell you *that*.

Laurie You're my sister, we shared a womb—

Thea We're not twins—

Laurie It was a *time*-share; how much money do you have?

Thea We have finished with this line of questioning. (*Beat.*)

Laurie Yes, you're right, forgive me.
    Listen, I *am* sorry about your trouble.
    Is it all right with you and Eamon? I mean, are things?

Thea We do our best.

Laurie It must be hard.

Thea It is.

Laurie If I can help.

Thea You do.

Laurie How?

Thea You listen.

Laurie I do do that.

Thea Sex . . . has become a little difficult.

Laurie I thought that happened more with women who were or had been actually pregnant—

Thea Yes—well—I think he's started to see my body as a sort of—broken machine; or something that rejects part of him that can't be—subsumed by me—or—oh, we've been hashing it out—and I think the self-consciousness of that has contributed to the problem. That had been such a special part of our lives. I miss it so much. I haven't told any of this to anyone else.

Laurie That's okay . . . what are we *for* if not to share that stuff?

Thea You're right.

Laurie How much money do you have?

Thea You're *such* a creep.

Laurie I knew it—

Thea You're such a creep sometimes—

Laurie It's the most intimate thing—it's the most important thing—

Thea That's ridiculous—

Laurie I'm right—

Thea You're absurd—

Laurie I'm just right—

    (*Eamon enters.*)

Eamon So that's good, so that will be nice, having Abby here. I haven't seen her in a year!

Thea Yes, it will be lovely.

Eamon Oh, that makes me happy!
    What were you two talking about?

Laurie Your money.

(*Pause.*)

Eamon (*Stiffly.*) What were you . . . *saying* about it?

Laurie (*He shivers.*) We were talking about its size.

Eamon Size?

Laurie The size of your fortune.

Eamon . . . Ah.
(*Little uncomfortable laugh.*) In what . . . sorts of terms? General or—

Thea He's lying.

Eamon I don't understand.

Thea He's being incorrigible.

Thea I didn't say anything.

Laurie (*Shivers.*) She didn't disclose the extent of your pelf, Eamon.

Eamon Oh. She's a good girl. *You're* a scamp! But that's what we like you for.

Laurie Every court needs its jes—

Eamon Why aren't you drinking?

Laurie I'd like some hot water and honey, actually?

Eamon You're shivering.

Thea I'll get it.

(*Goes off.*)

Laurie Slight cold. Nothing too—so Abby, what age would Abby be these days?

Eamon Lordy: seventeen.

Laurie Seventeen—God, you're old.

Eamon She was the product of—

Laurie A youthful indiscretion?

Eamon —An early marriage, bub.

Laurie Really? I thought the early marriage was a product of *her*.

Eamon Well, in either direction, I was twenty-*two*. So: not an old man yet.

Laurie No.
   You haven't seen her in nearly a *year*?

Eamon She's been away at school.

Laurie She's a freshman at Princeton, is it?

Eamon My *alma mater*.

Laurie Well, that's far.

Eamon Not so far.

Laurie Fifty-five minutes by—

Eamon She's come into town; she's just . . . not much chosen to see *me*.

Laurie Well: Kids. (*Shivers.*)

Eamon You sure you don't have a fever?

   (*Touches his forehead.*)

Laurie Just a cold.

   (*Pulls away.*)

Eamon Your forehead's damp—

Laurie I'm unctuous; I'm sure she loves you.

Eamon Who? Abby? Well . . . I was young to be a father. I hope next time . . .

(*Trails off, smiles sadly at Laurie.*)

Laurie Um, so listen, Thea didn't tell me a word about your money, but she gave me a detailed account of your various relations to her *womb*—and—

Eamon She did?

Laurie Yes—and so if you want someone to talk . . .

Eamon I'm glad, I'm glad she did, I was hoping I could *talk* to you about things—

Laurie Well. Sure.

(*He shivers.*)

Eamon This has been very hard on us—very deleterious—I like to think that our love—is a strong enough thing—the fiber of it, you know—and it isn't as though the passion had faded—it hasn't—but I find it hard—I find it hard to accomplish what I need to, if you know what I'm saying—and it tears at me as a man and a husband.

Laurie Was there—was that what happened—some version of that—in your first marriage?

Eamon With Abby's mother?

Laurie Did pregnancy have some sort of effect on—

Eamon Oh no, with Abby's mother it'd pop up like you'd put a coin in a slot. To the day we divorced. The day *after,* truthfully.

Laurie Ah. So there the problem was just—

Eamon There the problem was just that the woman was a damnable fucking bitch; it was sexual thralldom, pure and simple: I was ruled by my member in those days.

I don't know what's going to happen.
Your sister and I . . . the nights when she would just hold me—by "me" I mean *it*, you know—

Laurie You Irish have such a gift of gab.

Eamon To think of that being over. *Over.*
Makes me suicidal.
When Thea came along . . . she was the first woman I'd met in years who wasn't starving. I looked at her and saw . . . a real life! With holidays and babies and a hearth . . .
(*Looks around wistfully.*) Maybe if I put in a hearth . . .
Not to have a child—the *chance* of a child who comes out right—what will my life have been?
God, no—this is a party night—Christmas!
I hope I haven't made you uncomfortable. I've been talking kind of freely.

Laurie Not at all.

Eamon You're a good friend, Laurie. Not just a brother-in-law.

Laurie I feel the same way.
Eamon?

Eamon Yes?

Laurie How much money do you have? (*Beat.*)

Eamon You know what you are? A *monstre sacre*! A *monstre sacre*—that's you!

Laurie Is it?

Eamon Yes, indeed.
Say, so have you seen your friend Oliver's play?

Laurie Uh. Yes.

Eamon We loved it. So charming.

Laurie Yes.

Eamon What a one he is, that one, eh? *So* talented! *So* successful! And so *kind*!

Laurie Uh-huh—

Eamon And not bad-*looking,* either—

Laurie —No—

Eamon And I don't mean just for a *writer*—

Laurie No; even for people he's—

Eamon And he loves you, you know; *God,* he loves you—

Laurie Yes, I know. It's peculiar in a—

Eamon (*Overlaps.*) It's almost peculiar the way—yes "Peculiar"—I think the same word—but you must be so happy for his success.

Laurie Uh-huh.

Eamon It must be so nice when a close friend in your own profession succeeds so spectacularly.

Laurie It's what you do it for—

Eamon Mind you, in business, we wouldn't be so generous; but business seems to me a more egoistic world than the arts.

Laurie Absolutely—

Eamon Because you're all so in touch with your humanity all the time, there must be much less pettiness, I envy you that.

Laurie Well. Do.

Eamon Well, I do. So you must be—what is the word Thea always uses? The Yiddish word? "Kuhfeeling"—

Laurie That sounds so weird in an Irish accent: "Kvelling," probably—

Eamon "Kuhfeeling," that's it.

Laurie Well—no—that's not—quite, but yes, I am "kuh-feeling"—or what is that word the Irish use—means almost the same—"keening"—I'm "*keening*" is what—

Eamon No, "keening" is for funerals and wakes—

Laurie Because I loved the play so much. So much. Do you know what I think of the play? I think Oliver's play is *The Cherry Orchard* if *The Cherry Orchard* actually *worked*. I think it's a little bit better than *Macbeth*, *much* more touching than *Endgame* and very nearly as accomplished as *Plaza Suite*. No, I really do.

Eamon Ah.
   (*Beat.*) Then have you seen any *movies* you've liked lately?

Laurie I don't like things, Eamon, don't you know that?
   I'm a savage, bitter man, with a lump of coal where my heart should be.
   (*Beat.*) No, I did like that *one* movie—

Eamon Which one was that?

Laurie I can't remember the title for some reas—, but it was about *resting*.

Eamon Resting?

Laurie Yes. And I liked it for that reason. Because I've never seen a movie about resting, before—or anything else, for that matter, and I think it's a terribly important issue.

Eamon Resting is?

Laurie Yes. Resting is, I think, at the bottom of everything in a way. We toil through our days, through our countless *tasks,* always with the aim in mind of some *ending.* Of *rest.* And yet, when we *do* rest—or approximate it—we panic—we plunge into the most morbid depressions—we can't stand it you see—it's too—existentially quiet—too deathward—and so this film—about lying in hammocks—

ostensibly—caused me to question the most basic premise of my existence.

Eamon Which is?

Laurie That I am working like hell in the vain hope of making enough money that I can pass the day unconscious.

(*Pause.*)

Eamon Anytime you want to use the house—

Laurie I need a break—but I can't think where to go—

Eamon The house is there—it's sitting there, Laurie, you can stay there year round—we'll pay the heating bills, et cetera, you needn't worry about that—

Laurie I can't be alone in your house—

Eamon Why not?

Laurie Because, Eamon, have you never realized that that house is *spooky*?

Eamon It is?

Laurie I keep thinking Ichabod Crane is going to walk in.

Eamon We'll build you another one.

Laurie I'm exhausted.

Eamon Anything we can do.

Laurie You're a good man.

Eamon You're kin.

(*Thea enters, on the phone, carrying hot water for Laurie.*)

Thea Uh-huh—well *good*—well that's *fine*—

Laurie Listen, don't tell Thea I got—

Eamon Not a bit, lad.

Thea We look forward to seeing you—yeah, bye—we've missed you, too.

Terribly. Painfully. Yeah, bye.

(*Hangs up.*) That loser friend of yours from college, Max, is coming to the party. Did you invite him?

Eamon He must have gotten wind—

Thea Christ, Eamon!

Eamon He's a good fellow—

Thea He's changing careers again.

Eamon The acting isn't working out.

Thea Neither did the teaching—neither did—didn't he work for you, once?

Eamon Briefly, Thea—it's just coming to a party; what can happen . . . keep a civil tongue with him?

(*The door buzzer.*)

Thea That must be Mom and Dad.

Laurie Fashionably early; oh God.

Thea (*Crossing.*) Eamon, I'm going to kill you—
Mom? Dad? Is that you?

Laurie Is Max the painter?

Eamon No, he's—oh yes! That's him!

Laurie He's a bad painter.

Eamon No longer.

Oliver (*Offstage.*) It's us; I'm sorry we're early.

Thea Oliver, hi!

(*We hear her unlatch the door, a dog barks. Oliver and the dog enter. The dog is enormous.*)

Oliver Merry Christmas! Hey! Have you all met Thunder?

Eamon No. Hello Boy.

(*Gia enters. She is eight months pregnant and carrying a baby in swaddling and baby duffel. Thea follows, stricken. Gia speaks in a thick, lyrical Italian accent.*)

Oliver I hope you don't mind—I brought everybody.

Gia I hope you don't mind.

(*The baby cries, shrieks.*)

Gia Ssh-ssh-ssh-ssh-ssh . . .

Oliver (*To Laurie. Opens his arms to embrace him.*) Hey, bud.

Laurie Don't touch me, I have a cold.

Oliver What are you talking about?
(*Holds him, kisses him.*) Merry Christmas.

Laurie Hello, Gia.

Gia Hello, Laurie.

Oliver Have you said hi to Thunder and Amos?

Laurie (*To dog:*) Hello, Amos.
(*To screaming baby:*) Hello, Thunder.

Oliver We just thought *they* deserved Christmas, too. I hope it's okay—

Gia Is there place we can put the baby?

Thea You can toss him on the bed with the coats.

Eamon There aren't really separate rooms—just joggles and alcoves—

Laurie This apartment was commissioned by a white rat—

Thea I didn't know you were pregnant?

Gia *Que dice?*

Oliver (*Slowly and loudly.*) She said: she didn't know you were going to have another baby.

Gia Oh yes, yes . . .

Oliver It was sort of an accident—it happened the first time we had sex after Amos—

Gia (*Holds up a finger.*) *La prima volta dopa por Amos.*

Oliver Thunder, you okay boy?

Gia Babies babies babies—(*She laughs.*)

Oliver Is there a post I can hitch him to, somewhere?

Eamon In one of the bed areas—right around here—

Oliver Thanks—

(*They go off.*)

Gia (*Coos Amos calm with quiet, charming Italian baby prattle. She looks up, smiles at Thea and Laurie.*) Hello.

Thea Can I get you something to drink?

Gia No, no—my milk—I cannot—

Thea Oh.

(*Gia gets lost in making faces at the baby and cooing. Then she moves, startled.*)

Gia Oh! A kick!

Thea Oh my God.

Gia (*Indicating her abdomen.*) The baby, you like to feel?

Thea No.

Gia (*Indicating Amos.*) The baby, you like to hold?

Thea No. (*She exits.*)

Gia Did I say . . . something?

Laurie Not in English that I could tell, no. (*An awkward moment while Gia—awkwardly— sits.*) How is your singing going?

Gia Oh. Yes. Um, well. The babies . . .

Laurie But you did come here to study, didn't you?

Gia Yes. To . . . study? Oh. Um. Yes. What?

Laurie . . . When is the next baby due?

Gia What does the baby do?

Laurie Sure, why not?

Gia Cry. Eat. Poop.

Laurie Ah!
  (*Beat. In the same mannerly tone:*) So what the fuck are you and Oliver about, anyway?

Gia . . . E-e-e-h-m-m . . . ?

Laurie (*Slightly louder and more distinct, still polite.*) I was wondering: What is the basis of your travesty of a marriage to Oliver?

  (*A look comes over Gia as if she's basking in sunlight, and when she speaks, it's from the groin.*)

Gia . . . Nnnnnn . . . Oh-lee-vair . . .

Laurie (*Wistfully.*) Yes. That's what I'd imagined.

  (*Oliver comes back, sits next to Gia, who puts an arm around him.*)

Oliver Eamon is amazing with his hands.
  (*Slap's Laurie on the knee.*) Hey, Bud, I want to get you alone.

Laurie For what reason?

227

Oliver We need to talk.

(*Gia holds the baby in one arm and with her free hand, strokes the back of Oliver's neck.*)

Laurie About anything in particular?

Gia Eamon amazing?

Oliver He's amazing with Thunder.

Gia How is Thunder?

Oliver He's really rassled him to the ground.
(*Thea enters with a bowl of nuts.*) I hope you don't mind: Thunder ate a table.

Thea A table?

Oliver Yes.

Thea Where?

Oliver In that lovely room with all the paintings. It was small.

Thea An *end* table?

Oliver I think so. Frankly, it looked quite old.

Thea It was.

Oliver I'm glad.

Thea Sixteenth century.

(*She exits with the bowl of nuts. Dog howls.*)

Oliver THUNDER, BE STILL!
(*The baby cries.*) Amos, honey, sh-sh.

Gia Sshh—sshh—sshh-sshh-sshh.

(*Amos cries.*)

Oliver Amos! Laurie, do you want to hold my baby?

Laurie No—I have a cold—

Oliver (*Placing him in Laurie's arms.*) Sure you do—

(*Laurie takes the baby, looks at him. The baby gets quiet. Laurie sneezes in his face. The baby screams.*)

Laurie (*In horror.*) I'm so sorry!

Oliver No problem, that's all right—

Gia (*In Italian.*) Oh the baby—look what he's done—my poor little Amos—how terrible, come here my baby I will make you better—the terrible man, using you like a handkerchief—

(*By now she's grabbed the baby from Laurie.*)

Oliver (*Overlaps.*) It's all right—it's okay—the baby's fine—

Laurie What's she saying?

Oliver (*Quite earnestly.*) I don't know, it's in Italian.

(*Buzzer sounds. Eamon pokes his head around the divider, holding the end of a leash. He's obviously being tugged at with enormous force.*)

Eamon Could somebody get that? (*He's yanked off-stage.*)

Thea (*Enters daubing at her eyes.*) I'll get it—Mom? Dad?

Sumner (*Offstage.*) Y-e-e-e-s!

Laurie (*To Oliver.*) Why don't we talk now?

Oliver Don't you want to say hi to your folks?

Laurie No, Oliver, that is the point—as long as humanly possible, I want to delay saying hi to my folks.

(*Laurie and Oliver start off to the kitchen cove. Sumner and Reva enter the room.*)

Sumner This goddamn city.

Reva (*Perpetual motion, perpetual speech.*) Ugh—this is the last time I come here. Who needs it? Hello, darling, mwa, don't let your father tell you about finding the parking space; it's a Russian novel, do we just throw our coats in the usual? Fine! Ugh! The trip in! One thing gentiles know how to do is tie up traffic, are you giving me your coat Sumner, or, *fine*! *Do* it yourself!
  (*RE: chair.*) This—not for sitting—but the place really looks surprisingly—(*She's now in view of Thunder.*)
  (*Thunder barks.*) OH MY GOD, IT'S A BEAR!
  (*Reva passes out. Thud.*)

Thea Mom?

  (*Lights black out.*)

  End Act One, Scene 1

Scene 2. (*Lights up on the kitchen. OLIVER and LAURIE enter.*)

Oliver But why *not*? I don't understand!

Laurie Ollie—

Oliver They must be such wonderful people—you *sprang* from their *loins*.

Laurie Not—can we—please: "loins"?—

Oliver I *have* to meet them.

Laurie Later.

Oliver Do you promise?

Laurie When everyone's napping.

Oliver I'm holding you to it—
  (*Starts stalking around the place.*) Look at this kitchen! Have you *eaten* here?

Laurie Maybe once or twice—no, once—

Oliver A place you've eaten. Describe it.

Laurie Oliver, that's sickening.

Oliver I can't help it. I want you to talk and talk and talk about the most mundane things, the way you do in your novels. I soak it up like an elixir!

Laurie Does one *soak up* elixirs?

Oliver (*Overlaps.*) I have missed you so terribly.

Laurie I had assumed that.

Oliver I feel it as an emptiness, an ache.

Laurie (*With him.*)—an ache; thank you. I've missed you, too. (*Shivers. Oliver lunges at him.*) *Don't hug me, I've* got a— (*Oliver hugs him, Laurie sneezes.*)—cold. You had warning.

Oliver You can snot on my shoulder anytime you want, darling—

Laurie I can't actually imagine *wanting* to—

Oliver I adore you.

Laurie I like you very much, too.

Oliver *Why don't I ever see you?*

Laurie Well—

Oliver How long has it been?

Laurie I don't—

Oliver I feel your absence in my *corpuscles*—

Laurie Yich.

Oliver O-o-h-h, look at you: all rumpled and sneezy and pretending to be unhappy the way you do, it's so adorable. I KNOW YOU THINK THIS IS UNGAINLY. Well, it's your own fault. I'm not like this in my real life. In my real life, I'm grim. You make me want to *live*.

Laurie That's sadly ironic, isn't it?

Oliver Laurie?

Laurie Yes?

Oliver I am having the most *shattering* success.

Laurie I—

Oliver It's like one day I woke up and a tsunami came knocking at my door—

Laurie A tsunami? Knocking? Really?

Oliver Laurie . . . I'm famous!

Laurie . . . Ummm—

Oliver I mean, I'm *hugely* famous.

Laurie U-h-h-h—

Oliver Well, I mean I'm not *fam*ous—in the *real* sense of the word—but in that tiny sphere where people care about what I do . . . I'm IMMENSELY famous.

Laurie Uh-huh.

Oliver And you're not around to share *every second of it;* that's so hard for me.

Laurie It's hard for me, too.

Oliver I know you've been busy. And I appreciate the phone calls—es*pe*cially when you pick up—and oh! If an *hour* spent with me were to mean that posterity might be robbed of a single *sen*tence you might compose—

Laurie Ollie, this is getting sort of creepy-sentimental—

Oliver The hell with it, I *am*! You have to get used to it.

Laurie Why is that?

Oliver Because that's how I am! It's my nature.

Laurie Well, it's your preference.

Oliver (*Delighted.*) What are you saying?

Laurie I have to get used to your romantic extravagance because that's "How you *are*"? I mean, is *lunging* at people and saying I ADORE YOU a kind of addiction, something you're not capable of modifying? Or is it just that you find it, what, *kicky,* so you're going to keep it up?

Oliver Do you not like it when I do that?

Laurie I . . .
   No, it's all right.
   Listen, are you going to adapt my book?

Oliver I was so flattered to be asked.

Laurie Oh, then you're turning it down?

Oliver Not on your life, Bud! The opportunity to run the words of a Laurie Weingard novel through my computer, how often does that come along in one lifetime?

Laurie Frequently in mine, and believe me it's no big thrill— is that *all* you're planning to do to it: *run* the words through your computer?

Oliver You have your *ideal* interpreter in me, Bud, because I am going to be as literal as verbatim as respectful as possible.

Laurie Just sort of . . . *copy?*

Oliver As much as I can.

Laurie And how much are they paying you for this feat of word processing?

Oliver . . . You know: an amount.

Laurie Which is . . . ?

(*Beat.*)

Oliver It's such a beautiful book, Laurie.

Laurie Ah.

Oliver I swear, I can't get through it without crying—

Laurie You can't get through your laundry without crying.

Oliver When I set out to be a novelist, it was because I'd read your first book—

Laurie The one that was well reviewed—

Oliver Yes. I thought, Holy Shit! That this is *possible* in a novel—

Laurie Having Cliff-Noted your way through the Classics—

Oliver In a *Contemporary* novel—
(*Delighted.*) Oh, you're bad, you're wicked, I've got to watch *out* for you—

Laurie Yes, you do.

Oliver So for me, ten years later, *not* having had success as a novelist, having enjoyed *enormous* success as a playwright, to adapt into a dramatic form even one of your *lesser* works, just has a rightness about it that I can't express.

Laurie I actually like that book best.

Oliver Oh! Absolutely! I just meant less popular.

Laurie That would describe *all* my books. Look, how far along are you? You wouldn't be nearly finished, would you, by some happy chance?

Oliver I'm having trouble coming up with an opening shot.

Laurie An *opening* shot?

234

Oliver Yes.

Laurie I don't understand—What's the problem?

Oliver Well—it's the way you write.

Laurie . . . There's something wrong with the way I—?

Oliver Oh darling—omigod—of course not! For a leisurely paced chronicle of rumination your style—

Laurie Oh dear—

Oliver —can't be beat. It's just that . . . well . . . your book is like the novels those *Eng*lish ladies write—where two hundred pages later they've poured the tea. I mean, it's virtually unadaptable. You see, it comes down to the differences between the media. You've got Theater, where I toil, which is *totally* irrelevant. Then you've got novels, which you do so magnificently, and which are totally irrelevant as well as completely ar*cha*ic. Then there are *movies,* which for the time being people are still going to, and therefore unlike those other *media* have to have some vitality. And I'm thinking that if I can just trump up a really strong opening shot, it'll trick people into thinking something is going to happen in the story. Which, of course, it does not.

Laurie What kind of opening shot . . . do you mean?

Oliver Chaos.
  Something chaotic.

Laurie Chaotic.

Oliver In a very *phy*sical way: Some kind of tangible mayhem.

Laurie Uh-huh.

Oliver Which is *hell,* because, as you know, your characters practically don't have bodies.

Laurie *Don't* they?

Oliver No.

Laurie That's a problem.

Oliver No, it isn't!

Laurie That they don't have bodies is not a problem?

Oliver In one of *your* books? Of *course* not! I mean: what would they *do* with them? They have *minds*.

Laurie (*Almost a plea.*) And *hearts*?

Oliver They have *minds*—they have *words*!
   It's the *most* beautiful book, Laurie—I swear, I can't—

Laurie (*Not kindly.*) I saw your play.

   (*Beat.*)

Oliver Gulp.

Laurie I'm sorry it took me so long to get to it—I never had a free night.

   (*Oliver has closed his eyes and put the flats of his hands against the table to steel himself.*)

Oliver . . . Okay . . . Okay
   (*Beat.*) Okay okay . . .
   (*He gulps.*) What do you think?

Laurie What do you think I thought?

Oliver I'm shitting a brick.

Laurie Oh baby, why?

Oliver Yours is the only opinion I care about.

   (*Beat.*)

Laurie You should have heard me talking about it before.

Oliver With whom?

Laurie Eamon.

Oliver I'm in agony.

Laurie Suffice to say, I compared it to *The Cherry Orchard.*

Oliver *Chek*hov's *The Cherry Orchard?*

Laurie *Ask* him. I compared it favorably.

Oliver That's over the top.

Laurie Yes, it is, but you know I ADORE you, so—

Oliver You really liked it?

Laurie Ask Eamon. Ask him to quote verbatim without insinuating inflections.

Oliver I can die now.

Laurie Yes. You can.

Oliver I can *die* now. I wrote this play for you.

   (*Pause.*)

Laurie (*Softly.*) Why?

Oliver Because I write all things for you. You're the voice in my head, my editor, my critic, my standard—someday I'm going to go back to novels—my dream is to write one as good as yours. And I know I never will. You're infinitely more talented; that's the fact.

   (*Beat. Laurie almost considers buying it.*)

Laurie If you actually believed that, you wouldn't be able to say it.

Oliver But I do believe it.

Laurie You certainly would not have conceived this weird, passionate, personal attachment to me; you wouldn't be *in love* with me this way—

Oliver If I weren't in love with you, I'd have to kill you.

Laurie God.

Oliver Baby, you're the most brilliant one. Everybody says it.

Laurie And I wish they'd stop.

Oliver Oh sweet man—

Laurie No, don't make it better. I know it's all you want, and you're incredibly sweet, really, but whatever you do, *don't* make it better. I want out of all that, Ollie. This—language of—bucking-up—and defenses shoring—

Oliver Laurie—

Laurie Here we are celebrating the birth of your Lord—and I am feeling dismally secular.

Oliver Are you *truly* unhappy?

Laurie . . . I want . . . something . . . I want . . .

Oliver What, sweetie?

Laurie I want—my perceptions to shift—I want—translation—transmogrification—transfiguration—
   (*Oliver holds him.*) I WANT MONEY!

Oliver Oh: *that*. Darling, take it from one who knows: you don't.

Laurie I do—*I do*—

Oliver Baby, you know how sometimes I speak in clichés?

Laurie Yes.

Oliver Here's one now: It doesn't buy happiness.

Laurie But it upgrades despair so beautifully.

Oliver Laurie—

Laurie I want money so I can be free from *thinking* about money—I want money so I can *buy* things—I want money so I can sleep all day—I want money so I can *live* on this *earth* since I have no relationship to *any other sphere*—

Oliver I know what you're going through—

Laurie I want it because I've stopped believing in any other thing—in any other substance—

Oliver With my baby and the new one and a wife—

Laurie Money is the purest, most solid connection we have to each other and the world—

Oliver I think about it all the time—but I have faith in God—

Laurie *Oh fuck you!*
(*Beat.*) I didn't mean that.
Oh Ollie, forgive me.
I'm going a little bit out of my mind.

Oliver Darling, you can tell me to fuck myself anytime you want. I don't mind that, but you're forgetting, and that makes me sad. You're forgetting the other things you believe in.

Laurie (*Hopeful for an instant.*) What other things?

Oliver Art. And friendship.

Laurie No.
Yes, of course. But the art is frustrating as much as anything and what are these friendships, anyway? Pleasant, and toothless, and built on flattery, and unlikely to survive the flimsiest test—

Oliver You know that is not the case.

Laurie I don't.

Oliver You *do*. And if you don't, I'm going to *make* you know it. I am your friend, Laurie, and I won't desert you no matter what test you put our friendship to. I will do *anything* to prove that to you.

Laurie Really.

Oliver Absolutely. Anything.

Laurie Anything'?

Oliver Absolutely.

Laurie (*Almost salivating.*) Tell me how much money you have.

Oliver The point is to get you off that topic.

Laurie Why?

Oliver Because it's not as important as you think.

Laurie Then tell me *casually.*

Oliver *Laurie.*

Laurie (*A throwaway.*) Okay. Show me your penis.

Oliver What?

Laurie Well, I can't imagine that would be much of a problem for you—denuding yourself. I mean, it's not *fiscal*—

Oliver Someone could walk in.

Laurie Oh, I guessed wrong.

Oliver Are you serious?

Laurie The question is, are *you*, Oliver? I mean, you *say* you can't *stand* my lack of faith. You *say* you'll do anything to prove your devotion. But when I ask you something so simple—something I'd *really* like to know, you refuse me. Which means all your highfalutin protestations are empty, doesn't it? Which has been my point all along, hasn't it?

(*Beat.*)

Oliver (*Slams his hand on table.*) By *God,* you're right!

(*Starts pulling off his clothes. Laurie has moved upstage to get more hot water and has his back to Oliver.*)

Laurie Of course I am. We all make attractive announcements and hope they amount to character, but when push comes to *shove*—

Oliver You're absolutely right, and this is not a problem.

Laurie (*Turning to Oliver.*) Oliver! What are you doing!

Oliver If this is what it takes—

Laurie Someone could walk in—

Oliver (*Overlaps.*) —then it's not a problem at all. Not at all—

Laurie *Stop!*

Oliver In fact, I hope this is just the first of *many* trials, Laurie. I want to muck out the Augean stables for you!

Laurie Jesus, I was right! I was *right!*

Oliver I just hope this will *prove* something to you. I just hope it will matter. Because I need you to have faith in something.
(*He's naked.*) There. What do you say to that?

Laurie (*Pause. Looks him up and down, stares at his penis, looks in his eyes.*) How much are they paying you to adapt my book?

Oliver I'm not going to say.

Laurie Why not?

Oliver Some things are private.

Laurie This is a curious moment to be telling me that.

Oliver I don't mind standing here before you like this. In fact, I think it's healthy for our relationship. I think it's a good idea for us finally to dive into the sub-current—the—choppy—the whatever-else-may-be-happening for *you*.

Laurie Oh, I can see where you might think that. Except—here's the thing—I'm not attracted to you.

Oliver You're *not*?

Laurie No. Although *this* moment has its interest, but . . . no.

Oliver That's so depressing.

Laurie Don't get me wrong—I might have had a moment across a crowded room and all— but then I got to know you—and care for you and that pretty much neutralized you for me. So if there *is* a "sub-current"—I think it trends in the other direction.

Oliver (*Quietly.*) Wow.

Laurie You see, I think we're opposites, Oliver, if you know what I—(God, this is weird, your sitting here like—)

Oliver (*Overlaps.*) Wow.

Laurie —In that, I find men sexually appealing but, with two or three exceptions—you're one—am bored to tears by them as people, while I really *like* women. Whereas you seem to be endlessly fascinated by the workings of men's minds but desire only women to sleep with. Which, I believe, is why you've married a woman who has no English and you call *me* "darling."

Oliver (*Delighted.*) You're amazing.

Laurie No, I'm not. And can your wife actually sing? No one's ever heard her.

Oliver She's getting better.

Laurie Ah.

Oliver This was *stun*ning.

Laurie Oh.

Oliver So much truth—

Laurie *The Iceman Cometh* in a three-million-dollar loft—

Oliver I am so grateful to you—

Laurie You're sitting there *na*ked.

Oliver I know.

Laurie You should be *pissed OFF*.

Oliver But I'm not.

Laurie Then something must be *wrong* with you.

Oliver (*Delighted.*) Something MUST be.

(*Sumner enters.*)

Sumner I want that dog killed.
(*Sees Laurie, not yet Oliver.*) You can't say hello?
(*Mock hostility masking real hostility.*) A father works his whole life, slaves, so he can bring up children, they can't even scratch themselves out of the kitchen, *nu?*

Laurie Hello, Dad.

Sumner Be grateful, some parents are really like that; what have you got, a cold?

Laurie Yes—

Sumner Your sister let a dog in the house—your mother fainted; I get a rest from her; is there water?

(*Looks around, sees Oliver.*)

Oliver Hi.

Laurie Dad, this is Oliver Elspeth.

Sumner The author! My wife and I loved your play. Very enjoyable.

Oliver (*Stands, shakes his hand.*) Mr. Weingard, I am so pleased to meet you. I want to thank you for your son, I *adore* him.

(*Sumner shakes his hand, looks at Laurie, exits.*)

Laurie Maybe you ought to get dressed.

(*Laurie's head sinks to the table. He passes out, and with him fade the lights. Lights up slowly, as his head lifts off the table. Reva in mid-speech.*)

Reva . . . dogs in the house all of a sudden?

Laurie I'm sorry?

Reva Do you know who brought the dog?

Laurie Um. Oliver.

Reva If I'd known.

Laurie Umm . . .

Reva But I'm disgusted with everything. Who's Oliver?

Laurie Um. Naked.

Reva What are you talking about?

Laurie What?

Reva You're a nutty.

Laurie Oh. Oliver is the good-looking one.

Reva (*Not happy with the description.*) What. Ever. (*Proud of it.*) I fainted.

Laurie Oh.

(*Lights flicker. Laurie stares out. Beat. Lights.*)

Reva (*Mid-speech.*) Anyway, I think it's in bad taste.

Laurie What is?

Reva The daughter.

Laurie Who?

Reva That Abby.

Laurie Is she here?

Reva Yes. I don't think that's right.

Laurie She's Eamon's daughter.

Reva But not your sister's.

Laurie And that makes it in bad taste for her to show up?

Reva And on Christmas!

Laurie They're Christians!

Reva I can see it makes your sister tense.

Laurie We're Jews!

Reva Listen, I can never say anything that pleases you; I won't even try—but that other one—that friend of Eamon's—

Laurie Max—

Reva *That* one.

Laurie Did he get here? How long have I been in this kitchen?

Reva He's so *scruffy* for an American!

Laurie He's Eamon's friend.

Reva Whereas Eamon is very well-scrubbed for a European—

Laurie I'm feeling . . . blurred—

Reva But I'm disgusted with everything these days—everything—

(*Laurie's head sinks to the table. He passes out, and with him fade the lights. Lights up slowly, as his head lifts off the table. Reva in mid-speech.*)

Reva (*Mid-speech.*) . . . and he hasn't improved at all.

Laurie Who?

Reva "Who?"

Laurie Oh.
Well, you married him.

Reva What does that mean?

Laurie I'd rather not be your confessor in this situation anymore—

Reva I have to talk to *some*body—

Laurie But to *me*?

Reva I don't have anybody else—

Laurie That's just *weird*.

Reva It's *him*. People come into the room, they see me, it's a pleasure; one look at him, you'd think somebody yelled "Fire"—

Laurie I know he's this small packet of hell, Mother, but you don't take responsibility for anything—and I think you actually *believe* you're completely innocent of—

Reva Listen, I am the only person I know who is not self-deluded and I have *never* done *anything* wrong.

Laurie I can't stand it!
Listen, listen—you *chose* him, you know. Oh—look—look—it's practically the new year, and I am sick, literally

246

grown physically ill with endorsing people's visions of themselves. And I know you can't redeem the past. So the only principle I can muster is to—give some zest to the here-and-now—for which you really need a lot more money than I possess but that's another story—but despite all that, I cannot any longer support your—willful anhedonia—this—mythology of victomology you've—

Reva An-hi-*what*-ia?

Laurie —committed yours—huh?

Reva What's that word?

Laurie What? Oh. "Anhedonia." It's the inability to experience pleasure. And what I'm saying is—

Reva Where did you get that word?

Laurie Mother, I'm a *writer*.

Reva Where did you hear tha—?

Laurie *It was the original title of Annie Hall!*
   But what I'm saying *is* . . . Look at yourself; you're still young—your mind—has certainly not di*mini*shed any, you've never been *sick* a day in your life, you're strong as a bull—I think after the nuclear holocaust all that'll be left will be a cockroach, a few southern women, and *you*. And yet you carry on as if everything had ended before it started! I mean it's not as if you're some babushkaed woman of Minsk! Other people in your situation rose above. Got divorced—made careers. My God, to hear you talk—your mother—history—your husband—all conspiring to wreck your life—and you there like—a leaf with nerve endings! Blown about—absorbing pain—well, you were *part* of it, too, and you very well may have *caused* some pain into the bargain—and if you would accept that—if you would only, only accept that you had a role in your own *life*—there might still be time—to be happy about something. I'm sorry, but this is the truth.

(*Pause.*)

Reva He was going to call it, "Anhedonia"?

Laurie Oh, Jesus.

Reva That's even worse than one of *your* titles.

Laurie *Mom*—

Reva Did you say you need money—

Laurie I'm fine.

Reva You said you needed—

Laurie I'm all right—

Reva We'll *give* you money!

Laurie Mom, stop!

(*Pause.*)

Reva But you'll tell us if you need money.

Laurie . . . I'm fine. I'm old.

Reva But you know you can always ask.

Laurie I *do*.

Reva Don't be shy, Laurie—

Laurie I'm *not*; I'm getting by.

Reva Where is your salary coming from these days'?

Laurie I don't make a salary.

Reva Your money— you *know* what I mean—

Laurie I have a lot of sources—

Reva I just wish you could have a hit.

Laurie They don't call novels hits, mother.

Reva A best-seller—you *know* what I'm—

Laurie I don't really *want* one, Mother—

Reva I couldn't even read John Grisham's last book.

Laurie I couldn't even read his first.

Reva He's a terrible writer.

Laurie I know that—I also know where this is heading—

Reva And yet everyone seems to want to read his books—at the library you have to reserve them months in advance.

Laurie Ah.

Reva You could write as badly as he does if you tried.

Laurie Actually, I can't.

Reva How do you know?

(*Pause.*)

Laurie (*Flat; a confession.*) I've tried.

(*Beat.*)

Reva Do you need—

Laurie I—!
No. (*Beat. Quietly at first.*)
There are . . . other substances, you know. There really are. You've always *had* a . . . certain amount of money, you've been "Comfortable" as you put it, yet you've passed your life in a marriage that's like a Saturday morning cartoon written by August Strindberg. Did your money get you out of that? Or get you anything. What? What? WHAT HAS IT GOT YOU? This *comfort*? This comfort you tout—it seems to me there is no comfort in it . . . anywhere. I will *die* before taking your money.

Reva (*Pulls back a little.*) I don't know why you keep *hoching* me. I just want you to have what Thea has.

Laurie (*Shivers.*) Thea has nothing.

Reva You're shivering. Take off your coat.

Laurie That's illogical.

Reva You'll catch a cold.

Laurie I *have* a cold.

Reva What. Ever.
So do you *talk* to your sister?

Laurie What does that mean?

Reva What could that mean? I want to know if you talk to her.

Laurie . . . Yes.

Reva What do you talk about?

Laurie . . . Things.

Reva Like what?

Laurie . . . Stuff.

Reva So, are they planning to have children?

Laurie Why do you ask?

Reva I'm an old woman, I'd like to have a grandchild before I die.

Laurie Oh, dear.

Reva Since I'm not holding my breath for *you* to have children anytime soon.

Laurie Oh—

Reva I've accepted it.

Laurie Mother, I'm the only *boy* who was ever named after a character in *Little Women,* what did you expect?

Reva Be quiet— I don't want your father to hear this part.

Laurie I suspect he may have caught on by now.

Reva No. He hasn't.

Laurie Oh, you know, I think he's probably read one of my books, at some point.

Reva Never all the way through.

(*Beat.*)

Laurie What?

Reva Agh, he's an idiot, I'm disgusted with everything—

Laurie He doesn't read them all the way through?

Reva In his defense, they're not so easy to get through.

Laurie Oh, well—there's *that*—

Reva It's hard for me to understand why you would choose to write books that are neither popular nor acclaimed.

Laurie I'm a writer's writer, Mother.

Reva What does that mean?

Laurie A failure.

Reva Well, that's what I'm saying; but getting back to your sister, why aren't they having children when they have so much to give?

Laurie You mean love?

Reva That, too.

Laurie I can't imagine.

Reva What is she waiting for?

Laurie I suspect she simply doesn't want children.

Reva Doesn't want them? Why not?

Laurie I suspect because she doesn't want to carry this conversation into another generation.

Reva Why *not*?

Laurie I can't imagine.

Reva I don't understand what you're telling me.

Laurie Don't you, Mother? Don't you, *really*?
  (*Silence. Laurie looks away, sighs, regretful.*) O-o-o-o-h-h, I didn't mean to . . .
  I try to give some zest to the here and now . . .
  It's just . . . I wish I could live with *facts,* do you know? Instead of . . .
  I don't even care what the facts are. I'm no optimist, I already suspect the worst . . . but to *know* it!
  If I could just say—with complete certainty—things are like this and like this and like this . . . and it's all incredibly bleak . . . it would be wonderful.
  Do you know'? Instead of all this . . . haggling . . . and pretending.
  (*No reaction.*) Mother, what does Jewish scripture say about an afterlife?

Reva Who?

Laurie Because I'm not grounded in this, and I wonder: what's the point-of-view?

Reva We don't think about it.

Laurie No?

Reva We certainly don't *talk* about it.

Laurie . . . Oh.

Reva We find this world to be enough.

Laurie . . . Ah.

Reva Too much, almost.

(*His head sinks with the lights. Lights up on Thea and Eamon in furious whispering.*)

Eamon . . . He's not the only reason your party is a disaster—

Thea I was not talking about the *party*, Eamon. I don't think the party is a disaster—oh, well, great, now you've given me something else to obsess about—

Eamon He is my oldest friend in the States, Max is; he was the first person not to make fun of my accent—

Thea He has no right to make fun of anything—to make fun of something you have to be superior in some way—and he's inferior in all ways—

Eamon He happens to be rather a brilliant man—

Thea He's drunk—he's leering—he's groping people—

Eamon It's *Christmas*.

Thea Oh, so that's the correct behavioral pattern for the occasion? Noel, Noel, grope, grope?

Eamon You might try extending a little bit of charity to him—

Thea He's dangerous, Eamon—

Eamon What can he do?

Thea I don't know but I know I'm right—

Eamon He's my friend—

Thea He's a nightmare— he's a *chaos*—

Eamon He's a *pal*—

(*Gia comes in with crying baby.*)

Gia Oh. Hello. I need to milk the baby.

Thea Please do it somewhere else!

Gia Thank you.

(*Stands there bewildered, smiling.*)

Thea La. In fondo, per favore.

Gia Yes, yes, thank you.

(*She exits. Thea cries.*)

Eamon Thea . . . Darling.

Thea Don't . . . talk . . . for a minute . . .

(*She cries. Laurie has been awake through all of this, but with half-lidded eyes.*)

Eamon It's all about another thing, isn't it?

Thea No. I hate him.

Eamon But there's the other. The other as well.

Thea But I hate him.

Eamon Thea, the man has been my friend far longer than you have. He has been loyal to me even as I grew rich and his life fell apart. And that's a loyalty harder to maintain than in the other direction. I can't abandon him just because he's catastrophic. Besides, this is all about something else.

Thea It isn't.

Eamon My daughter is in the next room glowering at me, like the history of my sins in*car*nate; your parents sit there inveighing against a dog; there's a pregnant woman virtually lactating into the punch and . . . I don't know what I have . . . any longer to hold onto. I *fail* . . . I *fail* you . . . daily.

Thea (*He kneels beside her, she holds.*) Eamon . . . I'm so sad . . .

Laurie I'm awake . . . by the way . . .

Thea That's all right. You fell asleep, sweetie. You're sick.

Eamon That's all right, Laurie. Take care of yourself.

Laurie (*His eyes shutter.*) If there's . . . anything I can do.

Oliver (*Enters.*) It's midnight. It's Christmas.

(*Lights flicker, as Laurie bobs and weaves, attempting to stand.*)

Reva (*Enters.*) The goyim want to toast the holiday like it's New Year's; I say let them!

Sumner (*Enters.*) Are there any nuts?

Gia (*Enters.*) Merry Christmas—

Reva You've had enough nuts.
(*To Oliver.*) Where's your dog?

Oliver You don't have to worry. He's in that beautiful octagonal space.

Thea Octagonal?

Oliver With those witty plastic statues.

Thea They're glass.

Oliver Oh. Are they'?

Eamon Let's have a toast then—Where's Abby? Where's Max?

Thea Who *cares*?

Gia In the next room.

Thea With the *coats*? Doing *what*?

Gia (*Searches briefly for the word.*) . . . Fucking.

(*A huge sound of shattering glass. Thunder barks.*)

Laurie (*Stands.*) Merry Christmas, Thunder.

(*Laurie collapses. Blackout.*)

End Act One

ACT TWO

(A hospital room Laurie in hospital gown, hooked up to an I.V. Thea is with him. Sumner sits by the window, in shadow reading a newspaper. Lights up: Thea mid-speech.)

Thea Which was the end of Christmas in one fell swoop. Darling, am I tiring you?

Laurie No.

Thea How are you feeling?

Laurie U-u-u-u-u-h-h-h . . .

Thea That's how you look. So tell me, have the doctors said anything new?

Laurie Not today. The nurse's aides or nurse-ettes or whatever they are—the vein-prickers—say they hate me at the lab; some days they stay open just to run my tests. They took fourteen vials of blood this morning.

Thea Astonishing.

Laurie Good morning, we need fourteen vials of your blood.

Thea Does the human body *have* fourteen vials of blood?

Laurie Not anymore.

Thea There must be nothing but carrot juice left in your veins.

Laurie If that.

Thea Along with the milk-of-human-kindness of course.

Laurie Oh, don't mock me, I'm genuinely ill.

Thea So have they suggested a *name* for what you have?

Laurie No.

Thea Laurie, it's been a week.

Laurie The doctors come in, their faces go white, and they scream, "God, you look like shit!" Thank you, I could get that from my friends. They're at a complete diagnostic impasse. They tell me I'm a fascinoma.

Thea What's a facsinoma?

Laurie It's a medical term; it means, "I trained in Guadalajara."

Thea These doctors are idiots.

Laurie I don't give a shit what I've got really, as long as I get out by Monday. I gave them a deadline, I said, Monday. They said, we'll *see*—

Thea Complete idiots.

Laurie I mean, who do they think they *are*?

Thea Trust me, darling, you're in *ter*rible hands.

Laurie I said, I'm *out* of here New Year's Eve—

Thea Well—

Laurie I said, look, you're *doctors;* do what you always do— treat the symptom! They looked *wound*ed. I mean, I'm lying here—corpsey—and I'm supposed to be concerned about their *feel*ings.

Thea Well, you disappointed them.

Laurie How?

Thea They were so excited when they thought you had AIDS.

Laurie Oh.

Thea I said, "Oh, please, what, from a *toilet* seat?"

Laurie Thea—

Thea I mean, even a spermatozoon gets a one-in-ten-billion shot at the target—

Laurie Please—not in front of Dad.

Thea . . . What?

Laurie (*Whispers.*) Although, at this point, I don't think it makes much difference.

Thea Sweetheart—

Laurie But still—

Thea Dad isn't here.

(*Beat.*)

Laurie Why are you doing this to me?

Thea Where do you think Dad is?

Laurie Oh, come on.

Thea Tell me where you think Dad is.
(*Laurie points to Sumner.*) Darling?

Laurie What?

Thea That's the air conditioner.

(*Laurie looks again, sees the air-conditioner, which is near Sumner, kicks off the bedclothes in frustration and buries his head in the pillow, with a cry.*)

Laurie The drugs they give me—my eyes go crazy—

Thea I know, sweetie—

Laurie All morning I thought the phone was a puppy: I kept waiting for it to bark—

Thea (*Covering him.*) Darling, cover up.

Laurie I don't want to—it doesn't feel good—

Thea I know, sweetheart, but you're a little bit exposing yourself—

Laurie That's because they make you wear these ludicrous togas!

Thea I know, but still.

Laurie They won't let me wear what I want.

Thea I'll make them, sweetheart, I'll talk to them; what do you want to wear?

Laurie A nice blue suit.

Thea Darling, you don't own a nice blue suit.

Laurie I thought this would be a good excuse to get one.

Thea No, sweetheart.

Laurie *I want to wear a nice blue suit!*

Thea You *can't.*

Laurie Oh God . . . How many people were in my graduating class in college? Eleven hundred?

Thea Something like that.

Laurie And I will bet you that of all those eleven hundred, I am the *only one* who doesn't own a blue suit.

Thea That isn't true.

Laurie It was a prestigious school—

Thea Still, they don't all own blue suits—

Laurie How do you *know* that?

Thea Because *some* of them are *dead*!

(*Beat.*) Now, why don't you drink a little orange juice?

Laurie It isn't juice, it's *gouache*.

Thea The sooner you ingest something, the sooner they'll let you out. They won't let you out, manacled to an I.V.—

Laurie I *have* to get out by New Year's Day—can you talk to them—can you *persuade* them—

Thea That's not realistic—your liver has shut down, your kidneys are barely functioning—

Laurie I've got *symptoms,* but they don't fit any *disease.* Just tell them it's psychosomatic; I'm a writer, tell them it's a metaphor—

Thea Why you've picked this arbitrary date—

Laurie Thea, I get evicted on January first.

(*Beat.*)

Thea Oh. That.

Laurie I get evicted unless I make it to—the court of Sanctioned Usury or Reading Gaol or wherever these things get taken care of, and obtain a Stay of Execution. Which will give me six months to figure something out.

Thea Laurie.

Laurie Six months to find another source—I can't be sick—I can't lose this time—

Thea Have you gone mad? Have you lost your mind?

Laurie I'm going to lose my home.

Thea It's been taken care of.

Laurie . . . How?

Thea Your business manager is our cousin.

Laurie Oh.

Thea Lucky for you. No one else would have you. A percentage of your income is tantamount to zero—

Laurie He told you'?

Thea Of course.

Laurie That's a violation of professional ethics.

Thea It's *family*. It's taken care of.

Laurie By Eamon.

Thea By me.

Laurie You don't have any money.

Thea I'm married to a rich guy.

Laurie It's *his*.

Thea And what's his is mine and what's mine is yours—

Laurie And God bless the child that's got his own. Thea, I can't have Eamon supporting me. It's wrong and it's tenuous.

Thea There's nothing tenuous about Eamon's money, Laurie; trust me, it's like the pyramids.

Laurie But your access to it depends on your marriage remaining intact, and from what I've seen, forgive me, but that's a pretty iffy proposition.

Thea There are things you haven't seen.

Laurie But you don't *work*.

Thea Eamon is generous in ways you don't understand. What makes him happy is to give me things.

Laurie I know that but—I'm sorry—after a while that *palls*. The most passionate, glorious, smothering people want something *back* eventually—or they feel like *tricks*—

Thea I've given him a lot back, Laurie—

Laurie —but you haven't given him a baby and you haven't taken a job, so basically what you've become is a hostess in a loft, and that gets *stale*.

Thea He loves me.

Laurie I don't *question* that. But to be a rich guy and *stay* in love with a woman who doesn't really, well, *do* anything—I think that would take a miracle.

Thea (*Unperturbed.*) Love is a miracle.

Laurie *And* an *econ*omy. And I don't want to start relying on the idea that my problems will be solved by the geyser of your great love trickling down on me. I . . .
  (*He passes out. Revives.*) Thank you.

Thea You're welcome.

Laurie Thea, I'm having a little trouble sorting things out.

Thea I know, darling.

Laurie Did something happen on Christmas? It's vague.

Thea Like what?

Laurie With you and Eamon . . . or with Abby and Max?

  (*Pause.*)

Thea I'm going to let you get some sleep.

Laurie Oh. Thea, if they decide to make Oliver's adaptation of my book, I get a production bonus.

Thea Good.

Laurie I'll pay you back, when that happens.

Thea If it happens, fine.

Laurie It'll be a decent amount of money.

(*His eyes start to shutter.*) If it happens . . . I'll be able to live for a while . . .

Thea This is not the time to think about all that, sweetie. You can rest now. We're going to take care of you . . . if you let us.

(*She kisses him and exits. Sumner looks up from his newspaper.*)

Sumner So, what, do you need some money?

(*Laurie looks at him. Lights. Sumner is still reading the paper. Eamon sits beside Laurie, kissing his forehead.*)

Eamon I'm not certain, but I think the fever may have diminished.

(*Laurie shivers violently.*)

Laurie I think so, too.

Eamon Laurie, shall I get you someone?

Laurie No, that's (*Shivers.*) over.
(*And suddenly it is.*) You know, the nurses come in wearing moon suits, they refuse to breathe my air; it seems I may have something fatal and communicable. I don't know why they let you all in, in your mufti.

Eamon Well, we're family.

Laurie (*Looking at Father.*) Why does this room have such a big air conditioner in December?

Eamon It doesn't seem so big to me.

Sumner What's that?

Eamon Does the air conditioner look big to you, Dad?

Laurie Oh.

Sumner No. Perfectly regulation size.

Eamon It's not so big, Laurie.

Sumner If you don't mind, I'm going to stretch my legs.

Laurie That's fine.

Sumner Can I get you people something from the cafeteria?

Laurie God, no.

Eamon No thanks, Dad.

Sumner I'll be back in a few minutes.

(*He sits there and continues reading the paper. A moment.*)

Eamon Truthfully, I'm glad he left. I wanted to talk to you, if that's all right.

Laurie Please.

Eamon I wanted to tell you about something that's happened—that nobody else knows about yet—only I don't want to burden you, I don't want to presume on your illness.

Laurie I would welcome a change of subject, frankly.

Eamon Oh, Laurie, I've come through the most hellish time; I've never had one like it before.

Laurie You mean with Thea?

Eamon Oh no. Oh no. Thea is perfect. She's incapable of doing anything that doesn't give me pleasure. Our situation— our problem is something else again—but Thea, herself, is a miracle.

Laurie Oh.

Eamon It's everything else . . . made me wonder . . . how I could be such an idiot.

Laurie Is this . . . your daughter?

Eamon Oh.

Laurie And your friend?

Eamon Oh.

Laurie Is it about them fucking . . . on Christmas . . . on the guests' coats?

Eamon Only indirectly.

Laurie Really?

Eamon That was just the beginning . . . That I forgave. She's . . . a woman, now, after all, my daughter and he's . . . (*Starts to become teary.*) my oldest friend . . . and if they want to fuck . . . (*It's getting difficult.*) . . . if they want to fuck . . . well, isn't it nice that two people . . . whom I care for . . . take to each other so well? Isn't it?
   (*His eyes fill. Laurie hugs him. Light change; Eamon's tone suddenly sharpens.*) No, but it wasn't that—it was after. The letter that came.

Laurie What letter?

Eamon From them. Co-composed.

Laurie Do you have it?

Eamon No, I burned it.
   Laurie, it was nothing but bile . . . venom; it was an account of my wickedness, the evil of—

Laurie You have no wickedness in you, Eamon.

Eamon I didn't *think* I did . . . but it seems I must.
   I thought I was all right, but that must have been *pride*.

Laurie They're just shits.

Eamon My daughter said I was buying her off because I wasn't capable of giving her love. I know I was a poor . . . inept father in many ways . . . but I *did* love her—Max said my handouts were a power ploy—But Jesus, they weren't handouts! They were, at *worst—gifts*; I even *hired* the man,

266

once, when he was between careers—I *hushed* it up when he *embezzled* from me—

Laurie He embezzled from you?

Eamon Yes! And he claims my silence was blackmail!

Laurie Eamon—

Eamon This *money*—this thing of money—seems to have eaten up my life and I didn't even see it! I've always believed I became rich because I cared so *little* for the stuff. It was a game I played well—risks I took cheerfully because there was nothing about it I minded *losing*—but it *destroyed* me—

Laurie No—

Eamon If I hadn't had money, I wouldn't have lost my best friend—I might still have my daughter—and I wouldn't be able to afford the never-ending, crushing, *futile* round of jerkings-off and implantations and spontaneous rejections that have threatened to make a *hash* of my marriage—

Laurie Eamon, you can't obsess like this. I'm sure things will get better.

Eamon But that's the thing, Laurie—they already have!

Laurie They *have?*

Eamon I've *done* something, Laurie—something so wonderful, so glorious—and I wanted you to be the first to hear of it, because you're the only one I'm certain will understand.

Laurie What is it, Eamon? What have you done?

Eamon (*Beaming.*) Laurie—I've given away all my money.

(*Pause.*)

Laurie NURSE!

Eamon Laurie—!

Laurie HELP!

Sumner What did he say?

Eamon Be still, you're exposing yourself—

Sumner Mitten Drinnen, he's giving away his money?

Laurie Eamon, my God, be sensible!

Sumner (*Shakes his head.*) Ugh, if I live to be a hundred I'll never understand people.

  (*Returns to his paper.*)

Eamon It's too late, Laurie—it's underway, I couldn't stop it even if I wanted to—and I *don't* want to. Very quietly—I've kept it out of the papers—I've been emptying my trusts—diverting the funds to hundreds of charitable organizations. I'm leaving us just enough to start over—just enough for two people to keep their coats on. I haven't told Thea yet—

Sumner Hasn't told his wife; *nu?*

Eamon I thought it would be better if she found out once it was *fait accompli.*
  It will be a large bit of news for her.
  But *joyous.*
  (*Pause. Smiles at Laurie. Who doesn't really smile back.*)
Have I been an idiot in a different way?

Laurie No, Eamon . . . I admire you.
  (*Beat.*) Eamon—thank you for paying my rent.

  (*Beat.*)

Eamon (*Blanches: Horror.*) Oh my God!

Laurie (*Aside.*) That doesn't sound promising.

Eamon I'll never forgive myself. It slipped my mind—it absolutely—

Laurie But—

Eamon I should be flogged—oh, Laurie—

Laurie But Thea told me *she* took care of it—

Eamon She *did*—

Laurie Then it's not a problem—

Eamon She said, "Eamon: pay Laurie's rent." That's how Thea takes care of things—I'm a scoundrel—I'm a rotter—

Laurie Listen—we have till New Year's Eve—

Eamon But that's passed.

Laurie What? When?

Eamon Last night.

Laurie I *missed* the new year?

Sumner We had a party here.

Eamon We were all here.

Sumner The nurses let you have chipped ice.

Eamon I'm sure . . . there's something I can still do—

Laurie I have no place to live!

Sumner Happy New Year!

Eamon (*Slapping his forehead punitively.*) *Fuck* me! *Fuck* me!

Laurie I have to take care of this!

(*Laurie starts trying to find ways out of the bed. Reva and Thea enter.*)

Reva Why do all the nurses come in here wearing space suits and we come in here wearing Bendels?

Sumner Shush!

Reva I'm not going to shush. Look, now the air conditioner is shushing me. This is what it's come to.

Sumner They're having a bad moment—

Eamon (*Quickly.*) No, we're not! Not at all . . .

Reva So how do you feel, Laurie?

Laurie I—

Reva Because you look just awful.

Laurie I'm fine.

Thea That's good.

Reva If you were all that *fine,* you wouldn't be here.

Thea Ma, leave him alone.

Laurie Listen, I need to go out*side*—

Reva You don't want to do that.

Laurie Oh, I do—

Reva Believe me, I've just come from the outside, and it has *nothing* to offer. Rainy, muggy—ugh, I'm disgusted with all of it.

Sumner What are you talking about? It's a beautiful day.

Reva Do not contradict me, Sumner.

Sumner Not a cloud in the sky—

Reva Oh, listen to him, going all pantheistic on me, like he's a pleasant person—do you believe this man? I can't say, "Hello" without him registering an exception—

Laurie (*Trying to detach I.V.*) Please don't have a pitched battle over the weather in my hospital room—how do I get this *off me*? Oh my head!

Reva (*Pushes him down.*) Lie down; you're not going any-where so fast.

Sumner Why are you starting?

Reva I am not the one who started. I may be the first to go *loud* but *you* started—

(*A cry of frustration from Laurie.*)

Sumner When? When did I start?

Reva Nineteen-fifty nine and you never stopped.

Laurie I need to get out of here *right away*—

Thea Your doctors won't let you leave—

Laurie Screw my doctors; they're rank incompetents.

Reva That's not true. You are getting the best medical care a certain amount of money can buy.

Laurie And I can't afford even *that*.

Thea It's not *up* to you, remember? Oh, you're forgetting, aren't you?

Laurie Oh but it is—it is up to me—

Thea What are you *talking* about?
(*To Mom.*) He's forgetting.

Reva They get kooky in the hospital.

Eamon He's not talking about anything, are you, Laurie?

Laurie (*Trying again to get out.*) Thea—you don't understand—you don't *know* yet—

Eamon Laurie—

Reva Pay no attention. He's just moribund. They get like this.

Laurie (*This stops him.*) I'm just what?

Reva Remember how Ceil was before she went that time?

Laurie I'm just . . . WHAT?

Reva Don't raise your voice.

271

Laurie I'm . . . *moribund*?

Reva *Calm* down—

Laurie Moribund? What do you mean, "mori—"?

Reva Don't scream—

Laurie How do you even *know* that word?

Reva It was the original title of "Manhattan"; now lower your voice!

Laurie I can't believe . . . you'd call me . . .

Reva If the shoe fits.

Sumner Reva! This isn't appropriate conversation—

Reva Thank you, Emily Post.

Sumner Look at the poor kid—you've made him nuts—

Reva Oh stop pretending, Mr. Charming-Public-Manners-But-Mean-As-Hell-At-Home. This is what I live with.

Laurie My *head*—please just be *pleasant*, okay?

Reva Pleasant? You want me to be pleasant? *I can't* be pleasant. You said so yourself. I'm incapable of experiencing pleasure. I'm suffering from Anatevka or whatever, I *can't be pleasant*!

Eamon Mom, would you like to come with me and get some coffee?

Reva I can't drink your people's coffee, it makes me sick the next day. Oh, I'm just disgusted with everything!

(*Reva stalks off to a corner.*)

Sumner Forty *years* of this woman.

Laurie Thea?

Thea Yes, darling?

Laurie Come here, would you?

Thea (*Coming to him.*) Of course, darling.

Laurie People are telling me *ev*erything, right? I mean . . . I'm not . . . moribund . . . am I?

Thea Certainly *not*.
(*She pats his head.*) . . . Of course, we don't really *know* anything, yet.

Laurie Thea—!

Thea And they *do* keep sending in that rabbi.

Laurie Thea?

Thea *Death*, though . . .

(*She lets it hang.*)

Laurie *What?*

Thea When you think about it, death . . . is really relative, isn't it?

Laurie No.

Thea I mean, it doesn't exist in itself, does it? It's just the loss of life. And you can only *lose* as much as you *have*. . . .
Darling, you've got nothing to worry about.

Laurie Thea!

Thea I mean, what is your life, really? Take-out dinners and Nick-At-Night?

Laurie I have my *work*.

Thea No now, sweetheart, I'm being *serious*.

Laurie So am I.

Thea It's not as if Eamon or I were going—*that* would be something—

Reva Now, that would be a lot of paperwork.

Laurie (*Blurts it out.*) Not anymore!

Eamon Laurie.

Laurie Not—any—*more*.

Eamon Uh, Laurie.

Reva What are you talking about? Their lives are very big. They have each other, they have money, there's still time for children knock wood—

Laurie They're not going to have children—

Eamon Uh, Laurie,

Laurie —because they *don't* have money.

Reva You're incoherent.

Thea This is the blood sugar talking.

Laurie No, Thea, it's not, it's the truth. You see, Mom, they're not going to have children because they're not capable of having children the old way, they're too self-impressed to adopt, and by the end of the week they won't be able to afford the new technologies because Eamon has taken a unilateral vow of poverty and is systematically scattering his fortune among random ostensibly worthy causes, leaving himself and your daughter only enough to keep their coats on; so, no, Mom, no money, no children, just each other. Fortunately, *love* is a miracle.

(*Stunned beat.*)

Eamon Oh, now, that was perhaps impulsive.

Thea Eamon?

Eamon Darling . . .

Thea Eamon, is this true?

Eamon I was meaning to break it to you over a quiet dinner.

Laurie You'll be eating Cuban-Chinese now.

Thea Eamon!

Eamon I thought . . . it would be better for us . . .

Reva You gave away your money?

Eamon I couldn't bear it anymore, what's happened . . .

Reva Like Mrs. Astor or somebody, handing out the Astor fortune to whatever charity comes knocking at the door?

Eamon All that's happened . . .

Reva *Mrs. Astor is a hundred-and-thirty-seven years old!*

Eamon I wanted it to be just *us* again . . . loving each other.

Thea (*In tears, hits his chest.*) You . . . dumb . . . *mick!*

Reva Oh, this is the end!

Sumner Reva—

Reva Don't start with me, Sumner. You gave away your money? You didn't even consult your wife? Ugh, I'm just disgusted with everything! Why are we still here? I want to go home! How long before this thing happens, anyway?

Laurie What thing?

Reva . . . Forget I'm here.

Laurie *What . . . thing?*
Oh my God . . . You want it to happen.

Reva What are you talking about?

Laurie Admit it. You want it to happen.

Reva Oh, you, you, you with your "admit its!"
You're supposed to be some sort of writer; is this what you really like? These big, passé, melodramatic scenes where

somebody tells a secret and everything changes forever? The way it never happens in real life or if it does, everything's forgotten by the time the fortune cookies get there?

You want me to "admit it"? Fine. I'll admit it. I *want* you to go.

And take your sister along with you while you're at it.

Why shouldn't I?

You're always upset with me, you're always mocking me. What am I supposed to be, grateful for that? What, the laws of people no longer apply to me?

Sumner Sh—

Reva Don't shush me, Sumner, I know what I'm talking about, and they like you even less, so ha-ha.

They're just waiting for *us* to die anyway—

Thea That's not—

Reva Oh, don't yell "no," I know what I'm talking about.

They can't even understand why we're not *eager* to oblige—why we don't leap at the opportunity to drop dead.

They ask each other: "Why are they reluctant? *We're* fine with the idea."

Well, let me tell you, it's not like you reach a point and you're fine with the idea. "Serene old age" was invented by a *forty*-year-old. The real thing is terrifying, it's physically painful and it's frankly depressing. Whatever may be torturing you now, *trust me,* you'll be *nostalgic* for when you hit your father's age.

So why lie?

Why pretend there isn't something attractive in the thought that you'll go first? And then Thea, God willing. Your father, there's no problem—look at the man.

Boom, boom, boom, the entire chain link fence of disasters that is my life tumbling like the Berlin Wall—like none of it ever happened.

And I start up again.

And maybe there's a shot at a *day* of—I won't say *happiness*—but *not awful.*
(*Silence. Reva goes to Laurie's bedside, tucks him in.*) How do you feel, Laurie? You look dreadful.

Laurie I . . . am not . . . *moribund!*

Reva Mori-*who?*

Laurie Moribund—!

Reva Of course you're not. Who ever said such a thing?

Laurie I am not *sick*!
I am not *dying*!
I have *health*!
I have *strength*!

Thea Laurie!

Laurie I have *money*!
(*Realizes it.*) I *have* money.

Eamon Laurie—

Laurie I HAVE MONEY!

Thea Darling, sit down!

Laurie O-LI-V-E-E-E-R!!!

(*Lights. When they come back up, Oliver is leaning over Laurie. Gia sits, hugely pregnant, rocking baby in her arms, and surrounded by baby duffel.*)

Hello, sleepyhead!

Laurie Oliver—you've come! Thank God. Thank you for getting here so fast.

Oliver I've missed you like crazy, my buddy. How do you feel, my sweetie?

Laurie My entire body is in excruciating pain.

Oliver (*Sagely.*) Ah, well, disused things grow sick.

Laurie (*Finding that overwrought.*) Blecch.

Gia (*Gingerly.*) Hello, how *are* you?

Laurie Oh, Gia! Well actually—I think I'm getting well.

Oliver Great!

Laurie Well, I think I'm getting well—

Oliver Fantastic—

Laurie Well, I think I'm getting well—

Oliver Pookie.

Laurie What?

Oliver Stop.

Laurie Oh.

Oliver It's like: At the Hospital with Gertrude Stein.

Laurie That sounds like something *I* would say.

Oliver Do they know what you have yet, baby?

Laurie No.

Oliver That sucks.

Laurie Yes.

Oliver Of course it's a boon to *my* schadenfreude, but from your perspective—

Laurie *That* sounds like me, too.

Oliver Look at this place! *Your* hospital room—a place where you've been sick!
 (*Takes out pad and pencil.*) Describe it to me!

Laurie Oh—Ollie—I need to ask you something—

Oliver No—You need to *tell* me things, darling—You need to tell me your secrets—you need to make me the heir to your secrets—

Laurie The heir?

Oliver Everything must look so *different* to you now—

Laurie No—

Oliver It *must*.

Laurie Not really.

Oliver I in*sist*.

Laurie There's this general feeling of profundity but it never turns into anything specifically interesting.

Oliver Wow! That's so interesting!

(*Writes furiously in pad. Amos howls.*)

Oliver Amos, shut up! I don't know what this mania for babies is, anyway, are they supposed to be redemptive or, as it usually turns out, merely repetitive?

Laurie Stop talking in my voice!

Oliver Why? You're not using it for anything.

(*He smiles.*)

Laurie Ollie, listen, I need you to pay attention to me, now.

Oliver That's all I ever *do,* darling.

Laurie No. What you do is point your face in my direction then *doodle* something but now I need you to *really see* me and understand, all right? Ollie, the most terrible . . . crushing things have been happening. I used to think the world was indifferent to my existence, but, as it turns out, it's actively opposed. The only thing that stands between me and ruin is your screenplay. So, Ollie, what I'm asking is: will you please, as my best friend, put everything else aside—all your other projects and your handsomeness and your famousness and your unique skill as an impregnator—and will you please *finish* that screenplay and save my life? *Will* you, Ollie? *Please?*

(*Pause.*)

Oliver Aw shit.

Laurie (*Aside.*) That doesn't sound promising.

Oliver I didn't want to tell you—

Laurie Tell me? Tell me what?

Oliver I didn't want to be the one to tell you—
The screenplay, sweetheart, the screenplay: it's
over.

Laurie ... Things get so garbled in my head. "Over" means what again?

Oliver I turned in my draft, they paid me off. They've stopped the project, Laurie, they've discontinued the project—it's never going to be made—it's over!

Laurie ... Then I am, too.

(*Silence. Gia interprets it.*)

Gia Oh! "Bye-Bye."

(*She starts out.*)

Laurie How did this happen, Ollie? *Why* did it happen?

(*Gia sighs resignedly, drops bag in place.*)

Oliver Because I fucked it up! Because I did a lousy, lousy, lousy job!

Laurie (*Almost consoling.*) Oh . . . Ollie . . .

Oliver And the terrible thing is? I did it on *pur*pose.

(*Slow lights up with Laurie.*)

Laurie . . . You—did it—on— You *did it on*—?

Oliver I sabotaged it, Laurie. In a way I wasn't conscious I was doing it—Shit! I'm lying! I was completely conscious I was doing it—CHRIST! CAN'T I EVEN TELL THE TRUTH WHEN I'M TELLING THE TRUTH?—
(*The baby cries.*) *Oh shut up!* Laurie, it was a compulsion, a deeply personal compulsion like a coup d'etat—

Laurie Are coups d'etat deeply personal compul—

Oliver I don't know why, I don't know what it was in me, YES I DO! The only way I can think to explain it is: Have you ever read that critic Harold Bloom?

Laurie Oh God, no, not Harold Bloom, not in Mount Sinai—

Oliver Because Harold Bloom has this theory—

Laurie (*Gnawing his pillow.*) G-R-A-G-H!

Oliver (*Continuous.*)—that all writers are locked in a battle to the death with their spiritual forebears, who are the Great Writers of the Past—

Laurie No more, no more!

Oliver —which makes total sense, except for one flaw, which is that it assumes we've actually *read* the Great Writers of the Past, which to a large extent I have not.

Laurie Please—I *beg* you—

Oliver To tell you the truth, I haven't even read Harold *Bloom*, just the articles about him in the glossy magazines—

(*A noise of suffering from Laurie.*) But they were enough for me to understand the nature of the Agon or struggle, I have been involved in with *you*—

Laurie Please . . .

Oliver —*You* being my substitute for someone really *great*.

Laurie *Please* . . .

Oliver I've had to overthrow you—it was a kind of love-death thing, do you see?

Laurie How could you *do this*?

Oliver I know—I know—You're my master—my con-science—my best friend—I love you—and I've betrayed you utterly—and my feelings about it are extremely *mixed*.

   Wow! I thought that would be hard, but, you know, it's really quite cleansing. (*He smiles.*)

Laurie Get out.

Oliver But I've con*fessed*.

Laurie *So?*

Oliver Don't you have to forgive me?

Laurie For*give* you? Because you've con*fessed*? When you haven't even said any *Hail Marys*?

   No—I do *not* forgive you, Oliver—I will never forgive you for this, you have *ruined* me—

Oliver But haven't you wanted to do the same thing to me?

Laurie I may have *wanted* it—I didn't *or*chestrate it!

Oliver Is there a difference, really?

Laurie Yes! Yes! Yes! All the difference! Jesus! I am not a *game,* Oliver, I am not a figment of your imagination, I am not a *chara*cter in one of your tepid and successful

plays. I EXIST! I am *sep*arate from you! ! You're a *thief*!
You've *taken* from me, YOU'RE A VAMPIRE! You've
sucked me dry! I AM REAL! I AM *SICK*! I AM . . .
BRO-O-O-O-O-KE!

(*He has started jumping on the bed.*)

Oliver What can I do to redeem myself?

Laurie (*Lunging.*) NOTHING!

Oliver (*Fending him off.*) I'll do anything—

Laurie GET OUT!

Oliver Laurie—

Laurie WHAT?

(*Oliver drops his pants.*)

Gia (*Natters in Italian.*)

Laurie Get out! Get out!

(*Laurie starts getting tangled up in his I.V Oliver scrambles
to pull up his pants, hustle his family out of the room.*)

Laurie (*Tangled in his I.V., howling.*) Go—go—go—

(*Continues with this.*)

Oliver (*To Gia.*) We're leaving—

Gia What?

Oliver We're going home, now—

Gia I am sorry?

Oliver (*Loudly, with gestures.*) We're leaving . . .

Laurie Go!

Oliver . . . the hospital . . .

Laurie Go!

Oliver . . . and taking a cab . . .

Laurie Go!

Oliver . . . home.

Laurie Go!

Gia Oh, yes . . .

(*They start out. Oliver stops again, so do Gia et. al.*)

Oliver Laurie . . .

Laurie . . . *What?*

Oliver Thunder died.

Laurie . . . Oh.

Oliver He was chasing a sparrow and got hit by a truck. Thunder's dead.

Laurie I'm very sorry to hear that.

Oliver Thank you.

Laurie *OUT!*

Gia Bye—Bye—

(*The Elspeths leave. By this point, Laurie is in a heap on the floor. Sumner looks over to him, sighs, puts down his newspaper.*)

Sumner Oy, look at you, you're exposing yourself.

(*He crosses over, kneels, helps him off the floor and onto the bed. Laurie expects his father to return to his chair, he doesn't.*)

Laurie Thank you.

(*Sumner stays beside him.*)

Sumner So I bet all your friends think I'm gay.
(*Laurie looks aghast.*) Well, that's how they think, isn't it?
Frankly I don't believe that's the answer.
(*Laurie look aghast again.*) Maybe I've had a fleeting
attraction or what-have-you but I don't think that's the
explanation. SO tell your friends from me they don't know
their ass from third base.

Laurie . . . Okay . . .

(*Beat.*)

Sumner Okay. What-have-you.
(*Beat.*) So, have you noticed? I'm here night and day—

Laurie Yes . . . Why is that?

Sumner "Why?" "Why?" he asks? My son is in the hospital
with an unknown disease and he wants to know why I'm here
night and day—

Laurie Oh—oh well, oh—

Sumner For a change of *pace*. I get cooped up in that apartment, with your mother, whom I really don't care for—that's
a joke. What do I do? I read the paper. I can do that here as
well as anywhere.

Laurie Okay.

Sumner If you want to know the truth, I think that was at the
root of it more than the sex problem.

Laurie What?

Sumner Cramped living quarters. We never could get the
right Feng Shui going—

Laurie I'm sorry?

Sumner Did you ever read Virginia Woolf's essay, "A Room
of One's Own"?

Laurie Yes. Did *you*?

Sumner It's an interesting piece, except I think it *errs* in its gynocentrism.

Laurie (*Shakes his head.*) Does it?

Sumner I never had my own room.

Laurie Oh . . .

Sumner In my whole life. I lived at home. Then the Army. Then home again. Where did I have my own room in that?

Laurie Uh; nowhere?

Sumner Correct. I married your mother. Our wedding night, I thought: Oh shit, at least before I had my own *bed*!
  This was the problem. Not the sex disappointment.

Laurie Oh.

Sumner We didn't expect much in that department. Sex, love; phooey. People wanted to live in their own houses. What did we expect? But sharing everything; this I wasn't prepared to do forever.

Laurie You should have built a little shack in the backyard.

  (*Beat.*)

Sumner (*Slaps his forehead.*) *Now* you tell me. Of *course*. It's funny that never occurred to me—

Laurie Well, you being a contractor and all—

Sumner You see, I was never enterprising, I never had ideas like that . . . a shack! Oh, well. Jeez. Too bad. You would have had a much better time.

Laurie Yes.

Sumner Because, contrary to popular opinion, before I started a family I was popular.

Laurie Really?

Sumner You see, I was a *loner*.

Laurie U-u-u-m-m . . . I don't follow.

Sumner I was extremely popular among people who didn't want to be bothered.

Laurie Ah!

Sumner I had *dozens* of intimate friends I hardly ever saw.

Laurie Oh.

Sumner It was a nice time. I was happy.

Laurie This was . . . when, exactly?

Sumner When I was happy?

Laurie Yes.

Sumner U-u-u-u-h . . . the late forties.

Laurie Oh. Yes. That would be right.

Sumner After that, no.

Laurie Oh.

Sumner The mistake was having children; but what can you do?

Laurie Nothing, I—

Sumner Once they come, they never leave—

Laurie No.

Sumner Marriage, if you're creative, you can get out of, but children—

Laurie I know—

Sumner Marriage is merely a prison; children: the *abyss*.

(*Beat.*)

Laurie I see.

Sumner But if I'd had a room, a shack! A shack! Go figure. Also your mother was no pleasure. Aside from the sex, which you don't need to know about—

Laurie Thank you.

Sumner She was a *congeries* of problems. First, she was from Brooklyn, while I was from the Bronx. This made her fancy. You know that type? Well. Just listen to her talk. That accent: Flatbush on the Thames. That should have been my warning. Fools rush in. Then there was her *reading*, her *pottery*, her with the card games all the time and so forth. Plus, she was always there. This was her highest crime in my book. So what do you do? You accommodate. You adjust. You know, very often, when I would explode, and insult you in public, and tell you you disgusted me and so forth, and then not talk for two weeks?—

Laurie Yes.

Sumner I didn't really mean it.

Laurie Oh.

Sumner It was just a way of keeping people out of the room.

Laurie Oh.

Sumner I want you to know. So you shouldn't get your feelings hurt.

Laurie Ah. . . . Timely.

Sumner What I'm *saying*—I'm saying, I did my best.

Laurie It wasn't very good.

Sumner I've come to accept my limitations in that regard. And you?

Laurie . . . The fact is . . . I don't deeply *care,* anymore.

Sumner How can that be?

Laurie I have so much else to—Oh, please—I mean, those people who the only thing that ever happened to them was that they were *reared* badly? Spare me. Things happen, it stops being significant. There are so many people to be disappointed by, you've become . . . quite beside the point.

Sumner You've got all these other people, and mostly who I've got is you.
　　(*Laurie looks at him.*) Ha-ha: Joke's on me.
　　(*Beat.*) You should call your friend and apologize.

Laurie Who?

Sumner The writer.

Laurie *Oli*ver?

Sumner With the immigrant wife—

Laurie Are you in*sane*? Have you lost your *mind*?

Sumner It's my o*pin*ion—

Laurie Are you *nuts*?

Sumner Maybe so.

Laurie He be*trayed* me—he *rui*ned me!

Sumner You should forgive people their shortcomings—

Laurie Is *perfidy* a *short*coming?

Sumner I'm just being practical—

Laurie In what way can *that* advice be construed as prac—

Sumner Some day, you're going to miss him.
(*Pause.*) Laurie, I'm here night and day.

Laurie I . . . know that.

Sumner So, I'm just wondering: In the aftermath, are you going to app*rec*iate this?
(*A moan from Laurie.*) It's a perfectly acceptable question.

Laurie Yes. I'll appreciate it.

Sumner And will you forgive me for everything else?

Laurie Of *course* not.

(*Beat.*)

Sumner A bigger person would.

Laurie I've come to accept my limitations in that regard.

(*Pause. Gia enters in a nurse's uniform. She still has her accent.*)

Gia Good morning.

Laurie Gia—

Gia Who?

Sumner This is your nurse. Sheryl.

Gia Beverly.

Sumner Ugh: my apologies. See what happens you get old?

(*Gia opens curtains. Sunlight streams in.*)

Gia It is a beautiful day.

Laurie Are you here to steal my blood?

Gia Not this morning, no. Now. Would you like a massage?

Laurie No. I don't like being touched.

Gia Shall I get you your breakfast?

Laurie I can't keep anything down . . .

Gia Do you want me to sing for you?

Sumner Oh! Yes! That would be very pleasant.

Laurie *Can* you sing?

Gia Oh, yes.

Laurie I thought that was an excuse—I thought, I thought you were just milking Oliver, I thought it was one of the big lies we keep—

Sumner Would you shut up and let the lady sing?
   Go, dear.

Gia (*Taking concert position.*) This is an Italian song from "Twenty-four Italian Songs and Arias."

   (*There's an arpeggio and a spotlight. She sings, "Nina." It is plaintive and beautiful. She finishes. Hospital light returns.*)

Sumner Oh, that was lovely. You must have had lessons.

Gia Oh, yes.
   I must go to my other patients now.

Laurie Gia—

Sumner (*Correcting.*) Dorothy—

Gia Beverly.

Laurie What was that song about?

Gia A sick dog.

   (*She exits. Laurie and Sumner are alone.*)

Sumner So. . . .
   Do you need money?

(*Pause.*)

Laurie Yes.

Sumner . . . Ah.
   May I *give* you some money?

Laurie Yes, daddy, you may.

End Act II

EPILOGUE

(*Thea and Eamon's apartment. A beautiful spring morning. Sunlight, flowers. Laurie stands with a glass of Coke. His blue suit fits beautifully, his hair is neatly combed, his color is excellent. He looks well. Thea is bustling about the apartment, refilling bowls, etc.*)

Thea Well, that all sounds wonderful, darling—

Laurie The best thing about it is the *clarity* I feel—

Thea I'm sure you do, darling, I'm *certain* of it—

Laurie About everything, you know. Not just physically better—

Thea The chemo isn't killing you?

Laurie No—it's nothing—

Thea You don't get sick—you don't throw up?

Laurie Nothing like that at all—it's quite amazing, really—of course, I get about a dozen antinausea drugs first—

Thea (*Crossing to far end of room.*) I'm so relieved—

Laurie Yes—but I mean—it's this clarity thing—

Thea Uh-huh—

Laurie I feel—

Thea I'M ON THE OTHER SIDE OF THE ROOM!

Laurie Oh, oh, then I'll—

Thea YOU'RE GOING TO HAVE TO SPEAK UP OR I WON'T HEAR YOU!

Laurie I DON'T FEEL LIKE SHOUTING!

Thea THEN I'LL COME BACK TO YOU!
(*She heads back.*) God, they're really kvelling over that new painting in there—even *Mom*—

Laurie The new Old Master, you mean?

Thea What. Ever.

Laurie And the five new rooms are quite something, too.

Thea I needed a project.

Laurie How can you afford all that anyway, at this point?

Thea Laurie, don't ask these kinds of questions—

Laurie I guess when Eamon talks about "enough money for two people to keep their coats" he's referring to *ermine*—

Thea So you feel clear?

Laurie I . . . do. Oh look, you know, I'm so so *so* determined not to learn anything from this experience.

Thea Are you as furious at your doctors as I am?

Laurie Um . . . not really—

Thea Because I'm still furious at them. Scaring us like that. When all you had was the most curable cancer known to man.

Laurie In my oncologist's office the other day, I was flipping through this back issue of *People* magazine—and there was this article about some television starlet who had exactly what I have—and they listed the symptoms. Precisely my symptoms, down the line—

Thea And they called you a fascinoma!

Laurie The next time I come down with anything, I'm not going to consult my doctor, I'm going straight to the editors of *People* magazine.

Thea It will save time, no question.

Laurie . . . I feel . . . good.

I don't know how to describe it . . . I don't know what the word for it is . . .

Thea Darling?

Laurie Yes?

Thea You're happy.

Laurie (*The color draining from his face.*) Oh God, I hope it isn't *that*.

Thea Sweetie.

Laurie It's just that . . . I think my whole life I've been trying to live with the facts, do you know? And here they were . . . and they were mostly horrible . . . and it was sort of . . . great surviving them, do you know?

I mean, God, there's still so much to work out—all the devastating things people said—obviously, that has to be dealt with at some point.

And I can't keep taking money from Dad, so there's money.

And I'm desperate to get to work on something—anything—because I haven't had an idea in months, and until I do, nothing will really count for anything.

But still I'm . . . happy.

Because the facts are out.

And it's left me with the most bizarre . . . wonderful feeling of clarity.

Thea You'll make the toast!

Laurie Oh Thea, I hate that sort of thing—

Thea When everyone's gathered, when everyone has a drink—

(*Eamon enters on phone.*)

Eamon Max and Abby are coming!

Thea (*Scowls.*) Oh good.

Eamon But *late*.

(*He exits.*)

Laurie That's weird.

Thea I can't even talk about it.

Laurie Eamon and Max have reconciled?

Thea I can't even discuss it.

Laurie After that e*piph*any Eamon had?

Thea It makes me sick.

Laurie (*Admiring.*) That Eamon.

Thea Which I should get used to because I'm having another go tomorrow.

Laurie . . . At . . . ?

Thea (*Sighs.*) Being a mommy.

Laurie Oh. Oh, Thea, oh really?

Thea It's going to work this time—I'm reading Norman Vincent Peale!

Laurie You're *not*!

Thea Don't yell at me, I even am. I couldn't bring myself to do the New Age crap, so I'm starting with the *old* New Age. It's garbage, of course, but I really think it might work. No, I mean: it's *going* to work.

Laurie I thought you were giving up on all that.

Thea I would but I can't remember the other things I wanted.

Laurie Thea—

Thea Be *happy* for me.

(*Sumner and Reva enter.*)

Sumner What a gorgeous painting, darling, I could look at it forever.

Reva Really beautiful. Let's go see this new room with the water—

Sumner God, I love paintings! I could look at art all day. Since I was a kid. I loved painting, I loved sculpture, I loved architecture. It was *people* I didn't have any use for. That's a joke.

Reva No, it's not. You're a horrible human being.

Sumner Why are you starting in?

Reva Don't *hoch* me, Sumner—

Sumner God, the way I'm always having to duck—

(*They're off.*)

Laurie You invited them.

Thea It's *Easter.*

Reva (*Off stage.*) Sumner!

Thea I'm bringing food!

(*Thea exits. Eamon enters.*)

Eamon Oh, I'm glad they're coming, Abby and Max!

Laurie That's amazing, Eamon. Considering what they did to you—considering how much it meant to you—

Eamon Well, it is a little hard to take, I'll grant you, when you find your oldest friend is fucking your seventeen-year-old daughter. Particularly the way it implicated everyone's *coats.*

Laurie I mean, the letter—

Eamon (*Continuous.*) But, you know, I believe he really *cares* for her. They're the wrong ages for each other. But, in a way, it's nice to find that two people I care for so much care for each other.

Laurie You really are remarkable, Eamon. First the money, now this. I admire you so much.

Eamon You're not drinking alcohol there, are you, Laurie?

Laurie No.

Eamon Thank God, you got me worrying—you can't drink and have your chemo, too!
    Mom? Dad? Can I bring you some food? (*He exits.*)

(*Oliver enters pushing a stroller.*)

Oliver Darling . . .

    (*Beat.*)

Laurie Hi.

Oliver Have you seen the painting?

Laurie Yes. It's very beautiful.

Oliver Wow. In their *home*. But the painting? Not as beautiful as you, Bud. Look at you!

Laurie Yes, I look nice. Oliver—listen—I need—I mean, I *want*—

(*Gia enters with the new baby. The duffel has doubled.*)

Oliver Hey! Have you met my new baby?

Laurie No—no—we haven't—met—

Oliver (*Picks up infant.*) Zeke, this is Laurie.

Laurie Hi . . . hi . . . Zeke?

Oliver Ezekiel Laurie Elspeth.

Laurie . . . Oh!

Oliver Are you surprised?

Laurie Yes. In Jewish tradition, we only name children after the *dead*.

Oliver Well, I know, but I thought . . . what the hell? *Risk* it.

(*Laurie hands the baby back.*)

Laurie He's nice.

(*The baby cries.*)

Oliver Oh Z-e-e-e-e-ke, shut up. This one cries worse than the other.

Laurie (*Suddenly.*) Oliver, I've forgiven you!

Oliver (*Moved almost to tears.*) You're a very great man.

Laurie No, I'm not. .

Oliver You've for*giv*en me!
May I ask what I've done?

Laurie . . . I—well—the *screen*play, of course.

Oliver Oh, that. I'm sorry about that—

Laurie I know—

Oliver It's just with the play and Amos and the new baby and Gia pregnant again, I haven't gotten around to starting it.

Thea *What?*

Laurie You haven't *STARTED* it?

Thea She's *PREGNANT* AGAIN?

(*Gia shrugs, smiles wistfully.*)

Oliver I know; we're freaks. But Laurie, I was thinking: maybe you and I could collaborate on the screenplay?

Laurie Collaborate?

Oliver I mentioned it to the three thousand producers and they were cool with the idea; we'd have to split the money, but that's still wow, a *lot*—

Laurie How much?—

Oliver Anyway, you must be itching to get back to work—

Laurie I am, but—

Oliver Who knows? Maybe you'll even come up with an opening shot—because frankly I'm still stuck—

Laurie But—wait—you *sabo*taged me—I—didn't you

   (*Gia comes up to Laurie.*)

Oliver What . . . ?

Laurie This is very confusing—

Gia Ehm, Laurie, may I speak a moment with you?

Laurie Um, yes, sure . . .

Gia (*Dismissing Oliver.*) Go. (*He goes. She turns back to Laurie.*) It is so good to see you no longer sick.

Laurie Thank—thank you—

Gia And I wanted to take this opportunity to express to you my gratitude for what you have done.

Laurie Your English . . .

Gia Ah, yes?

Laurie It's in English.

Gia Oh, yes, well, with the babies, I have undertaken to learn. Now Ohleevair and I can understand each other.

Laurie Oh, and how is that?

Gia Mmm, disappointing, *Ma,* this is what I must tell you! I am going back to conservatory to study my singing!

Laurie Oh good.

Gia Next week, I have an audition before the judges. I am going to sing for them and I am going to blow them!
   (*She beams at him. Reconsiders.*) *Away.*

Laurie Oh. Good.

Gia And it is all because of you.

Laurie I don't . . . understand . . .

Gia When I came into the hospital and sang the song, "Nina," for you—

Laurie The song about the sick dog—

Gia No, the song about Nina—

Laurie That *was* you—

Gia What you said after—

Laurie Did I say something after?

Gia —was so . . . encouraging and sagacious and lucid—

Laurie I don't remember any of this—

Gia It changed my life—

Laurie I don't remember *any* of this—

Gia And I must thank you so much.

Laurie Were you dressed as a nurse?

Gia What?

Laurie Did you call yourself Beverly?

Gia Eh?

Laurie Did Oliver sabotage my screenplay and is he just pretending?

Gia *Que dice?*

Laurie Did my mother tell me to drop dead? Did Eamon give away his money?

Gia (*Under.*) *Tu sei un pazzo.*

Laurie (*Continuous.*) Did my father say he had *fleet*ing at*trac*tions to *men*?

Thea (*Entering followed by Eamon and parents.*) Everybody gather round: Laurie wants to toast his clarity!

Laurie (*Taking her aside.*) Thea, I have to go!

Thea You can't go, darling, you have to make the toast.

Laurie I think I'm at the wrong party.

Thea You're the guest of honor.

Reva When are we having this toast already? Because these shoes: not for standing . . .

Laurie When I was in the hospital, did you tell Thea and me you wished we were dead?

Reva What!

Thea *Laur*ie . . .

Reva Are you in*sane*?

Laurie Well—

Reva I love my children. I would never say such a thing out loud.

(*Offstage crash. Thunder and Oliver bounce on.*)

Oliver Wait! Wait! Don't make the toast without us!

Laurie Thunder's alive, too?

Oliver Of course he's alive, Laurie, what did you think? Those beautiful blue vases, on the other hand—

Thea He broke the porcelain vases?

Oliver I know this artist who works in cement.

Reva What is it with you and that dog and the breaking?

Sumner Reva, leave them alone—

Reva Don't shush me, Sumner—

Sumner Reva, this is none of your business—

Reva Of course it is. When the children die, this all becomes ours. That's a joke, but no, seriously, I'm sorry but I'm going to have to kill that dog—

Oliver (*Quickly.*) I'll take him into another room—

Reva What other room? There aren't any left!
    (*Oliver trundles Thunder offstage. Everyone starts following.*) That animal has turned this apartment into Stonehenge! Don't talk to me, Sumner, your opinion is of no interest!
    (*Everyone starts squabbling—see appended monologues— eventually Thea and Laurie are left alone onstage, the arguing continuing off.*)

Thea Laurie . . . ?

Laurie Thea, how confused was I in the hospital?

Thea You were a little confused.

Laurie A *little*?

Thea For weeks, darling.

Laurie Oh.
    Then I don't know anything.

Thea That isn't true.

Laurie I thought I had the facts, but I made it all up, the way I always do.

Thea Not all of it—

Laurie I thought I was happy, but that was just an illusion—

Thea So is this—

Laurie There's nothing—I have nothing—no work—no money—no grip—just a boundless capacity for making mistakes.

Thea Mistakes are fine, Laurie, there's nothing wrong with—

Laurie Oh God! There's no way out of it! There's no way out! Why did I even bother getting well? It's horrible—

Thea No—it's wonderful.

Laurie There's nothing "wonderful," Thea—*I'm* a mess—*you're* going to make your ten thousandth attempt to get pregnant—it won't work—

Thea It will, this time—

Laurie —a mad canine is destroying all your things—

Thea We'll buy other things.

Laurie It won't matter! Don't you see that? You build these beautiful rooms and fill them with priceless objects and take the trouble to put them in perfect order—and in a flash a vast dog rips through and what are you left with? Nothing but mayhem! Chaos!

Thea There's more to it than that.

Laurie (*Hears the echo.*) Mayhem. Chaos.

Thea ... Laurie—

Laurie (*Seeing, setting the scene.*) A beautiful room filled with priceless objects in perfect order—

Thea Laurie, are you all right?

Laurie (*Growing excitement.*) A moment of stillness. Suddenly, a vast dog bounds onto the screen, shattering everything in its wake—

Thea Sweetie?—

Laurie From every corner, people emerge—passionately shrieking—mayhem! Chaos! *Oliver!*

Thea Laurie, maybe you should sit—

Laurie OLIVER!

(*Oliver races on, pulling the end of a taut leash.*)

Oliver I'm here, darling, I'm here, what is it?

Laurie Oliver—! I think I've found the opening shot!

(*Oliver throws up his hands in celebration. The leash whips offstage. The loudest crash yet is heard. Reva shouts, "OH MY GOD!" Offstage the people start passionately shrieking, the babies scream, the dog barks. Onstage, Laurie, Thea, and Oliver laugh. Mayhem. Chaos. Lights.*)

End of Play

THE MONOLOGUES:

Reva (*Continues from: "is of no interest. . . ."*) I mean, really, what is it with that husband of yours? I mean, I'm not saying he can't write, I found his play mildly entertaining, but who brings a dog out for an evening on the town? If you're talking to me, Sumner, I'm not listening, so why not save your breath because God knows you don't have any to spare. What are you, talking Italian again? So Berlitz is not all it's cracked up to be, is it? Sumner, shut up! But no, really, I think you really ought to work out some plan of reimbursing them. These are very expensive items your dog keeps eating and breaking and whatever if it *is* a dog because frankly I think it's a *bear,* at *least.* Sumner, why are you talking when I'm talking? Sumner, shut up! This very nice Italian girl with the meshuggeh husband and I are trying against all odds to have a conversation and would you please stop criticizing me who else would have stayed married to a thing like you all these OH I'M JUST DISGUSTED WITH EVERYTHING!

Sumner (*CUE: Reva speech: ". . . what's with that husband of yours"*) Reva, would you stop making such a thing of everything? Maybe they like having a dog breaking their art? Who are we to judge? It's not my bag, but the kids today are different. Plus, they have money like you never saw. People should do what they want to do and not have decrepit old people like us criticizing and hoching all the time. If they decide to buy the "Mona Lisa" and use it for *cat* chow, I say, *enjoy.* But to have to listen to your voice LEAVE THIS PRETTY ITALIAN GIRL ALONE to have to listen to your voice geshreing twenty-four hours a day, well, all I can say is in a past life I must have been Genghis Khan, because other-wise it's a nonsensical punishment. . . .

Eamon (*CUE: Sumner's speech "Who are we to judge . . ."*)
MOM—DAD—PLEASE.

No it's all right, Mom. It's all right, Dad. We don't mind.
I can afford it. It's just artists, they don't think of money and
art together. They don't think of money at all, so far as I can
tell, and when they see art, they don't value it, you see,
because they're all so talented they think that if art breaks
you can just go and make some new art. Which is quite
lovely, in a way, isn't it? But, no please don't start abusing
each other. It's Easter, and there's a ham, and we'll go out
and buy some new art tomorrow. If you'd just be quiet, you
don't want to go upsetting the baby to say nothing of the
dog. There are still a few things in the house that are break-
able. And that I love, so don't go working Thunder up, all
right? All right? OH FORGET IT! WHY AM I SO NICE
WHEN IT GETS ME NOWHERE? ABSOLUTELY NO-
WHERE. I'M A VERY WEALTHY MAN, I COULD HAVE
YOU ALL KILLED IF I WANTED! But can't you lower your
voices, really?

Gia (*In Italian. CUE: Reva speech. "found his play mildly
entertaining . . ."*) Oh, yes, I know, I'm sorry. What can I
do? The man is an idiot. I made a terrible mistake. Look at
him, superficially he's attractive, but he's crazy, he's crazy,
he has nothing to say, and he never changes his socks. I
don't know how you've managed to stay married as long as
you have because, frankly, I'm disgusted with everything.
You want to know a secret? The minute I get a couple of
good gigs, I'm going to (IN ENGLISH) "blow this pop
stand." I am taking the babies and getting a divorce. Well,
look at him—he's a lunatic. And I don't like the influence
he's had on Thunder. Thunder started out such a nice dog,
but now he's nervous around men and has a very uneven
sleeping pattern. That fucking Oliver! Also, I think he wants
to be homosexuals with your son. Oh! I'm just disgusted
with everything!

Thea (*CUE: Reva speech: "I mean, I'm not saying"*) Mom, Dad, can't we have one pleasant holiday? After all, we've got our health—isn't that enough? And Laurie's feeling well—shouldn't that make us behave? . . . Please. I love Easter. It's my favorite holiday!